Clockwise from far left: The Queen Elizabeth II Great Court, designed by Foster + Partners; the historic circular Reading Room, at the heart of the Great Court; exhibits in the museum's Egyptian collection; the museum's imposing main entrance

Expansion George II, George III and George IV added to Sloane's collection, as did other monarchs. Their gifts, combined with the Townley and Parthenon sculptures, burst the building's seams, and so architect Robert Smirke designed a new museum, completed by his son, Sydney, in 1857. Even so, with booty from expeditions and excavations pouring in, the natural history collections moved to South Kensington (▷ 38–39). When the British Library (▷ 67) moved to St. Pancras in 1998, the Great Court was redeveloped and the King's Library transformed into a gallery on the Enlightenment.

Modern spaces The £13-million World Conservation and Exhibition Centre opened in 2014, creating a spectacular setting for staging large-scale temporary exhibitions.

THE BASICS

britishmuseum.org

✚ J3

✉ Great Russell Street, WC1 (another entrance in Montague Place)

☎ 020 7323 8000

🕐 Sat–Thu 10–5.30, Fri 10–8.30

🍴 Restaurant, cafés

Ⓗ Holborn, Tottenham Court Road

♿ Very good

✋ Free, except for some temporary exhibitions

❓ Full educational schedule; free tours

HIGHLIGHTS

● The Queen's Gallery
● Changing the Guard
● State Coach, Royal Mews
● Nash's facade,
Quadrangle
● Gobelin tapestries in the
Guard Room
● Throne Room
● Van Dyck's portrait of
Charles I and family

TIPS

● To avoid the lines, book
a timed ticket in advance.
● Visit the quality royal
souvenir shops.

Of the capital's houses now open to visitors,
the Queen's London home is perhaps the
most fascinating. Where else can you see
a living sovereign's private art collection,
drawing rooms and horse harnesses?

Yet another palace British royals have had
homes across London over the years, moving
from Westminster to Whitehall to Kensington
and St. James's, and finally to Buckingham
Palace. It was George III who bought the prime-
site mansion in 1761 as a gift for his new bride,
the 17-year-old Queen Charlotte, leaving
St. James's Palace as the official royal residence.

Grand improvements King George IV and his
architect John Nash made extravagant changes
using Bath stone, later covered up by Edward

Clockwise from far left: Buckingham Palace is the London home of the British sovereign—the red, gold and blue Royal Standard is raised when the Queen is in residence; visitors at the palace gates; the Grand Staircase, designed by John Nash; the Mall, the ceremonial route to the palace

THE BASICS

royal.uk

royalcollection.org.uk

⊞ G7

✉ Buckingham Gate, SW1

☎ Tickets and information 0303 123 7300

⊙ Queen's Gallery: late Jul–Sep daily 9.30–5.30; Oct–late Jul daily 10–5.30; last admission 45 min before closing. Royal Mews: Feb–Mar, Nov Mon–Sat 10–4; Apr–Oct daily 10–5; last admission 45 min before closing. Check for occasional closures. State Rooms, Buckingham Palace: late Jul–Aug daily 9.30–7; Sep daily 9.30–6; last admission 1 hour 45 min before closing

🚇 Victoria, Hyde Park Corner, Green Park

🚆 Victoria

♿ Excellent

💲 Expensive

❓ No photography

Blore's facade added for Queen Victoria. Today, the 775 rooms and 16ha (40-acre) garden include the State Apartments, offices for the royal household, a cinema, a swimming pool and the Queen's private rooms.

Open house The Queen inherited the world's finest private art collection. The Queen's Gallery, completely refurbished for her Golden Jubilee in 2002, exhibits some of her treasures in changing exhibitions. In the Royal Mews, John Nash's stables house gleaming fairy-tale coaches, harnesses and other apparel used for royal ceremonies. Between late July and September, visitors can wander through the grand State Rooms resplendent with gold, pictures, porcelain, tapestries and thrones, and enjoy the gardens.

HIGHLIGHTS

- The Piazza
- St. Paul's Church
- Royal Opera House
- Shopping
- Markets
- Street performers

TIP

- Look out for blue plaques commemorating the famous people who have lived in the buildings, from writers (Charles Dickens, Jane Austen) to prima ballerina Dame Margot Fonteyn.

Buzzing with life and countless shops, bars, restaurants and the Royal Opera House, this vibrant area, with the Piazza at its heart, has elegant architecture and a long history.

Trading place When Inigo Jones laid out the Italian-style Piazza in the early 17th century, creating London's first residential square on what had been Westminster Abbey's orchard garden, traders supplied produce for the kitchens of the wealthy residents. As the market grew, the area became notorious for its noise, smell, drunkenness and prostitution until, in 1830, the purpose-built, colonnaded Market Hall opened. Housing London's wholesale fruit and vegetable market until 1974, when the market moved south of the Thames, the hall opened as a shopping center in 1980.

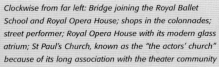

Clockwise from far left: Bridge joining the Royal Ballet School and Royal Opera House; shops in the colonnades; street performer; Royal Opera House with its modern glass atrium; St Paul's Church, known as the "the actors' church" because of its long association with the theater community

Church and music St. Paul's Church, built by Inigo Jones in 1633 and known as "the actors' church", contains interesting memorials and the graves of many noted Londoners. In 1662, diarist Samuel Pepys recorded Britain's first Punch & Judy puppet show in its portico, which is a popular backdrop for today's street performers. The facade of the Royal Opera House, home to the Royal Opera and Royal Ballet, dates from 1858; the interior was transformed by a £178 million building project in the 1990s and the Open Up project in 2015–18.

Beyond the markets The streets that fan out from the Piazza are packed with shops beloved by fashionistas and foodies who delight in discovering tucked-away corners like Neal's Yard (▷ 126) and nearby Seven Dials.

THE BASICS

coventgarden.london

✚ K5

✉ Covent Garden Piazza, WC2

☎ 020 7240 2992

🕐 Usual shopping hours Mon–Sat 10–7, Sun 11–4

🍴 Cafés, restaurants

🚇 Covent Garden

HIGHLIGHTS

- *Captain Augustus Keppel* by Sir Joshua Reynolds (Queen's House)
- Maritime equipment at the National Maritime Museum
- The Painted Hall, where Nelson's body lay in state after the Battle of Trafalgar
- Winter stargazing at the Royal Observatory

A UNESCO World Heritage Site, this historic district is a great day out, enthralling children and adults with science, sea stories and an excellent art collection. The town itself has a market, restaurants and a park.

Old Royal Naval College and the *Cutty Sark* Stop first at the *Cutty Sark*, once the world's fastest tea clipper. Ravaged by fire in 2007, it took five years to restore. Continue into the main quadrangle of the Old Royal Naval College. With your back to the Thames, the remarkable, recently restored Painted Hall, notable for its spectacular ceiling, is on the right.

Art and maritime heritage At the foot of Greenwich Park, the Queen's House and National Maritime Museum stand adjacent to

Clockwise from far left: The Cutty Sark; the Greenwich Meridian, the point chosen as 0° longitude; view of Queen's House and the National Maritime Museum from Greenwich Park; the Royal Observatory; the Galvanic Magnetic Clock, from which time around the world is measured

each other. The Queen's House is beautifully proportioned, but the real surprise is the outstanding art collection inside. The National Maritime Museum is crammed with hands-on exhibits and four galleries that opened in 2018 revealing the stories of epic global explorers. Boats on display range from small dinghies to the 7-ton *Miss Britain III*, the first powerboat to top 100mph (160kph). Don't miss the Asian treasures in the East India Company gallery.

Astronomical delights Inside Sir Christopher Wren's Royal Observatory, small galleries explain how time is measured. The astronomy galleries of the Planetarium next door merit even more time: they're modern, engaging and exciting, with regular high-quality screenings about the wonders of the night sky.

THE BASICS

visitgreenwich.org.uk
✚ See map ▷ 115
✉ Greenwich, SE10
🍴 Restaurants and cafés
Ⓓ DLR Greenwich, Cutty Sark
🚆 Greenwich, Maze Hill
🚢 From Westminster

Old Royal Naval College
ornc.org
☎ 020 8269 4747
🕐 Grounds daily 8am–11pm; Painted Hall, Chapel and Discover Greenwich Visitor Centre daily 10–5
♿ Good

The Queen's House, Royal Observatory, Planetarium, National Maritime Museum and *Cutty Sark*
rmg.co.uk
☎ 020 8858 4422
🕐 Daily 10–5; last admission 30 min before closing; Cutty Sark last admission 4.15
♿ Good (limited on *Cutty Sark*)

HIGHLIGHTS

- View of the building from Westminster Bridge
- Summer tours
- St. Stephen's Hall
- Westminster Hall
- Central Lobby
- Afternoon tea after a tour (advance booking essential)

TIP

- Big Ben is currently silent and swathed in scaffolding, undergoing renovation.

Britain is governed from this landmark building alongside the River Thames. For many visitors, its clock tower and Big Ben chiming the hour symbolize London. Interesting tours reveal its architecture, traditions and the workings of government.

Powerhouse for crown and state William the Conqueror made Westminster his seat of rule to watch over the London merchants. It was soon the heart of government for England, then for Britain, then for a globe-encircling empire. It was also the principal home of the monarchs until Henry VIII moved to Whitehall. Here the foundations of Parliament were laid according to Edward I's Model Parliament of 1295: a combination of elected citizens, lords and clergy. This developed into the House of

Clockwise from top left: A nighttime view of the Houses of Parliament from the South Bank; Thomas Thornycroft's early 20th-century bronze of Boadicea, by Westminster Bridge; Big Ben and the London Eye; Central Lobby, a meeting place between the House of Commons and the House of Lords

Commons (elected Members of Parliament) and the House of Lords (unelected senior members of State and Church). Henry VIII's Reformation Parliament of 1529–36 ended Church domination of Parliament and made the Commons more powerful than the Lords.

Fit for an empire Having survived the Catholic conspiracy to blow up Parliament on 5 November 1605, most of the buildings were destroyed by a fire in 1834. Kingdom and empire needed a new headquarters. With Charles Barry's plans and A.W. Pugin's detailed design, a masterpiece of Victorian Gothic was created. Behind the facade, the Lords is on the left and the Commons on the right. If Parliament is in session, there is a flag on Victoria Tower or, at night, a light on Big Ben.

THE BASICS

parliament.uk

➕ K8

✉ Westminster, SW1

☎ 020 7219 3000; tickets 020 7219 4114

🕐 Visits to House of Commons public gallery when house is sitting: Mon 2.30–10.30, Tue–Wed 11.30–7.30, Thu 9.30–5.30, Fri 9.30–3. Tours during summer recess (late Jul–early Sep) and Sat all year 9–4.15 (timed tickets). Audio and guided tours in many languages. UK citizens can arrange tours (and of Big Ben, when reopened) at other times through their MP

🚇 Westminster

🚆 Waterloo

💷 Parliament free; tours expensive

♿ Excellent

❓ Airport-style security screening in operation

HIGHLIGHTS

- First World War galleries
- Atrium: Witnesses to War
- Turning Points 1934–1945
- Family in Wartime exhibition
- Western Front trench
- The Holocaust Exhibition
- The Lord Ashcroft Gallery: Extraordinary Heroes
- Secret War exhibition
- Modern conflicts: Kosovo, Iraq and Afghanistan

Covering conflicts and their impact from World War I to the present day, this museum offers a thoughtful look at what life was like for soldiers and citizens, using personal objects, military might and testimonies from those who fought and those facing the challenges of life at home.

Extending its remit Originally conceived as a museum to collect and display material relating to the Great War, the Imperial War Museum opened to the public in the Crystal Palace in 1920. It moved to its present location, in what had been the Bethlem Royal Hospital (known as "Bedlam"), in 1936. By 1953 its remit had been extended to include all military operations in which Britain or the Commonwealth have been involved since 1914.

Clockwise from left: The impressive entrance and grounds of the Imperial War Museum; admiring the naval guns outside the museum; detail on an "Ole Bill" bus from World War I; tanks on display in the large exhibits gallery

New galleries A £40-million refurbishment resulted in the spectacular, much-enlarged First World War galleries, together with a redesign of the dramatic, four-story-high atrium, created by the innovative architecture and design team at Foster + Partners. The displays include a Spitfire, Harrier Jump Jet, V-1 "doodle-bug" and V-2 bombs suspended above field guns, and a T34 tank.

Created to coincide with the centenary of World War I, the galleries feature more than 1,300 original objects, including letters and diaries from the front line, interactive multimedia displays that give insight into life in the trenches and at home, and help visitors understand the war and its global impact. Among the objects on display are weapons, uniforms, keepsakes and trinkets, photographs and art.

THE BASICS

iwm.org.uk
➕ M8
✉ Lambeth Road, SE1
☎ 020 7416 5000
🕐 Daily 10–6
🍴 Café daily 10–5.30. Afternoon tea is served in the Park View Room
Ⓜ Lambeth North, Waterloo
🚆 Waterloo, Elephant and Castle
♿ Excellent
💷 Free; charge for some temporary exhibitions
❓ Full education schedules, talks and events

HIGHLIGHTS

- The King's grand staircase
- The Queen's state apartments
- Wind dial, King's Gallery
- Luminous Lace light piece
- Princess Victoria's dolls' house
- Royal dresses
- Tea in the Orangery
- The Sunken Garden

It's difficult not to be charmed by this royal residence with its grand state apartments, galleries and sunken garden—truly a fitting home for modern royals the Duke and Duchess of Cambridge, and Princess Eugenie and her husband, Jack Brooksbank.

Perfect location The year William III became king in 1689, he and his wife Mary bought a mansion in tiny Kensington village. William suffered with asthma, so the cleaner air here suited him, while the couple also wanted to be well placed for both London socializing and country living. Sir Christopher Wren and Nicholas Hawksmoor were brought in to remodel and enlarge the house, and they also later built the gracious Orangery for Queen Anne (with carvings by Grinling Gibbons).

Clockwise from far left: Princess Louise's sculpture of Queen Victoria in front of the palace; the King's Staircase; George Frampton's famed statue Peter Pan in Kensington Gardens; Princess Diana memorial garden; the Orangery

George I added palatial grandeur and the imposing King's Staircase, lined with life-sized figures from his court. George II's wife, Queen Caroline, created the Round Pond and Long Water to complete the 110ha (272-acre) Kensington Gardens. Today, trees are the backdrop for sculptures (such as George Frampton's *Peter Pan,* ▷ 72), monuments and contemporary exhibitions at the lakeside Serpentine Gallery and Serpentine Sackler Gallery.

New look A £12-million project has opened up previously unseen areas of the palace, including state apartments and landscaped public gardens. The routes focus on different historical eras and figures, including Diana, Princess of Wales, and Queen Victoria, whose story is told in her own words.

THE BASICS

hrp.org.uk
serpentinegalleries.org
✚ A6
✉ Kensington Gardens, W8
☎ 020 3166 6000
☎ Serpentine Gallery 020 7402 6075
🕐 Mar–Oct daily 10–6; Nov–Feb daily 10–4; last admission 1 hour before closing. Serpentine Galleries Tue–Sun 10–6
🍴 Kensington Palace Pavilion
🚇 High Street Kensington, Queensway
♿ Good
💷 Expensive. Serpentine free
❓ Personalized tours by expert Explainers

HIGHLIGHTS

● Food halls at Harrods
● Designer fashion at Harvey Nichols
● Boutiques on Walton Street

TIPS

● In Harrods, check out the day's events, shows and demos.
● Explore the side streets in the area to discover some interesting smaller (mainly fashion) shops.
● If it rains, stay put in Harrods and visit the spa.

Knightsbridge is London's smartest and most expensive neighborhood, with real estate, shops and price tags to match. It's the place for some serious retail therapy.

Stylish shops As you leave the Underground station (Sloane Street exit) you'll see Harvey Nichols (▷ 125), London's most fashionable department store. On emerging from Harvey Nichols, head back toward the Underground and continue along Brompton Road. Opposite is a huge Burberry store, known for its tan-and-gray check designs. On the left, as you walk toward the canopied shopfront of Harrods (▷ 125), is Swarovski, with its window displays of crystal jewelry. Leave Harrods by the Hans Road exit and you'll see luxury lingerie store Rigby & Peller across the street.

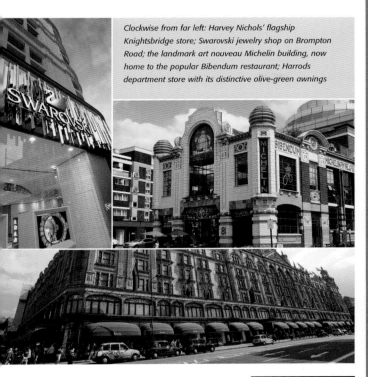

Clockwise from far left: Harvey Nichols' flagship Knightsbridge store; Swarovski jewelry shop on Brompton Road; the landmark art nouveau Michelin building, now home to the popular Bibendum restaurant; Harrods department store with its distinctive olive-green awnings

Even more stylish shops Return to Brompton Road and pass leather store Mulberry, before turning left into Beauchamp Place for smart restaurants, designer fashion and the Map House, with its antique maps and engravings. At the end of Beauchamp Place, turn right into attractive Walton Street, lined with interior design, jewelry and children's clothes shops. With Chanel to your right across Brompton Road, turn left into Sloane Avenue by the iconic Michelin building famed for its design, decor and Bibendum restaurant (▷ 145). The flag-ship Conran Shop, selling contemporary design for the home, is on the right. Continue down Sloane Avenue to reach the King's Road and The Shop at Bluebird, or turn left for Sloane Square, home to Peter Jones, the department store (▷ 126).

THE BASICS

✚ D7–E7

✉ Knightsbridge

🍴 Harvey Nichols' fifth floor is dedicated to food. Go to Harrods for elegant dining and macarons. The Berkeley Hotel, Wilton Place, tel 020 7235 6000, serves Prêt-à-Portea, a fashionista-themed afternoon tea (daily)

🚇 Knightsbridge

HIGHLIGHTS

● Panoramic views across
the city in every direction
● On a clear day you can
see for 40km (25 miles)
● Spotting landmarks along
the Thames
● Aerial view of the Palace
of Westminster

TIPS

● It is best to book ahead,
although not essential.
● Evening riders enjoy the
London lights.
● Tickets include access to
the 4D Experience, a 3D
film with special effects.

Attracting four million visitors a year, the
world's largest cantilevered observation
wheel soars 135m (443ft) above the
Thames, affording spectacular city views.

Riding high Passengers ride in one of the
32 capsules that rotate smoothly through
360 degrees in a slow-moving 30-minute flight.
Each capsule is fully enclosed and comfortably
holds 25 people. Because the capsules are
secured on the outside of the wheel (rather
than hung from it like a Ferris wheel), views
through the large glass windows are totally
unobstructed. Passengers can walk freely inside
the capsules, which are kept level by a motor-
ized motion-stability system—although seating
is provided. Each capsule is in touch with the
ground via camera and radio links. The wheel is

Clockwise from far left: Opened in 2000, the Eye quickly became an established part of the South Bank's landscape; the Eye at night; the glass capsules, attached to the outside of the wheel, offer unobstructed views; an aerial view of the Palace of Westminster at dusk

in constant motion, revolving continuously at 0.26m (0.85ft) per second, a quarter of the average walking speed, enabling passengers to walk straight on and off the moving capsules. After dark, the trees lining the approach to the London Eye are bathed in magical blue lights, while the boarding platform appears to float on a cloud of more blue light.

Revolutionary design Conceived by David Marks and Julia Barfield to celebrate the millennium, the Eye represents the turning of the century and is a universal and ancient symbol of regeneration. It took seven years and the expertise of people from five European countries for their design to be realized. The Eye is on the riverside Thames Path, which runs east all the way to the Thames Barrier.

THE BASICS

londoneye.com

➕ L7

✉ Riverside Gardens, next to County Hall, SE1

🕐 Daily 10am to mid- or late evening depending on time of year. Check website for details

🍴 Riverfront cafés

🚇 Waterloo, Westminster, Embankment, Charing Cross

🚆 Waterloo

♿ Very good. Boarding ramp available for wheel-chair users

💷 Expensive

HIGHLIGHTS

- London Before London gallery
- Hoard of 43 gold Roman coins
- Spitalfields Woman (Roman)
- Viking grave
- The lavish, late-18th-century Fanshawe dress
- Model of Tudor London
- Pleasure Gardens
- The London 2012 Olympic Cauldron gallery

A visit here is easily the best way to cruise through London's 2,000 years of history, pausing to see a Roman shoe or the Lord Mayor's state coach, or to peek through a Victorian shop window; it is even built on the West Gate of London's Roman fort.

A museum for London This is the world's largest and most comprehensive city museum, opened in 1976 in a building by Powell and Moya. The collection combines the old Guildhall Museum's City antiquities with the London Museum's costumes and other culturally related objects. The continuous building work and redevelopment in the City since the 1980s, allied with increased awareness about conservation, has ensured a steady flow of archaeological finds into the collection.

Clockwise from left: The opulent 18th-century Lord Mayor's state coach on display at the museum; a window to the city's past—the original museum building, built in the 1970s; coins from the second century AD, part of the impressive Roman exhibit

ANTONINUS PIUS
Emperor AD 138–61

A museum about London The building is, appropriately, in the barbican of the Roman fort, and the rooms are laid out chronologically to keep the story clear. The London Before London gallery follows the story of prehistoric Londoners before Roman settlement. One of the most impressive galleries is Roman London, which covers the period from the founding of Londinium in about AD50 until AD410, when the Roman army quit Britain. The Expanding City chronicles the Great Fire of 1666 to the 1850s, an era of wealth, power and global influence. People make a city, so in every room it is Londoners who are really telling the story, whether it is through Roman ceramics or Tudor clothes. A major redevelopment has resulted in superb displays and a mesmerizing re-creation of the 18th-century Vauxhall Pleasure Gardens.

THE BASICS

museumoflondon.org.uk
✚ P3
✉ 150 London Wall, EC2
☎ 020 7001 9844
🕐 Daily 10–6
🍴 Cafés, restaurant
Ⓜ Barbican, St. Paul's
🚆 Liverpool Street, City Thameslink, Farringdon
♿ Excellent
📷 Free; prices vary for temporary exhibitions
❓ Full education schedule; audio tour

HIGHLIGHTS

- *Virgin Enthroned* by Cenni di Pepi (aka Cimabue)
- The Burlington House Cartoon by Leonardo da Vinci
- *Portrait of Pope Julius II* by Raphael
- *The Arnolfini Portrait* by van Eyck
- *Equestrian Portrait of Charles I* by van Dyck
- *The Hay Wain* by Constable
- *Madonna of the Pinks* by Raphael
- *The Archers* by Raeburn
- *Sunflowers* by van Gogh
- *Mr and Mrs William Hallett* by Gainsborough
- *La Pointe de la Hève* by Monet

Britain's premier art gallery holds some of the world's most famous paintings and it's free to visit, so you can drop in for a few minutes' peace in front of *The Hay Wain* or Rubens' ravishing *Samson and Delilah*.

Quality collection Founded in 1824 with just 38 pictures, the National Gallery now has more than 2,300 paintings, all on show. Spread throughout William Wilkins' neoclassical building and the Sainsbury Wing extension, they provide a high-quality, concise panorama of European painting from Giotto to Cézanne.

Free from the start Unusually for a national painting collection, the nucleus is not royal but the collection of John Julius Angerstein, a self-made financier. From the start it was open to

Clockwise from far left: The gallery's impressive neoclassical facade, fronting Trafalgar Square; the East Wing was completed in 1876; a detail of Vincent van Gogh's 1888 painting Sunflowers

all, free of charge, and provided a wide spectrum of British painting within a European context—aims that are still maintained today. However, there may be a charge for the temporary exhibitions in the Sainsbury Wing.

A first visit To take advantage of the rich artistic panorama, choose a room from each of the four chronologically arranged sections. Early paintings by Duccio di Buoninsegna, Jan van Eyck, Piero della Francesca and others fill the Sainsbury Wing. The West Wing has 16th-century pictures, including Michelangelo's *Entombment*, while the North Wing is devoted to 17th-century artists such as van Dyck, Rubens, Rembrandt and painters of the Dutch school. The East Wing runs from Chardin through Gainsborough to Matisse and Picasso.

THE BASICS

nationalgallery.org.uk

 J6

✉ Trafalgar Square, WC2

☎ 020 7747 2885

🕐 Sat–Thu 10–6, Fri 10–9

🍴 Restaurant, café

Ⓜ Charing Cross, Leicester Square

🚆 Charing Cross

♿ Excellent

🆓 Free

❓ Guided tours (free daily 11.30 and 2.30), apps, lectures, films, audio guide, interactive screens. Free 10-minute talks (Mon–Fri 4pm), free lunchtime talks (days vary, 1pm)

HIGHLIGHTS

● *St Rémy Self-portrait with Barbara Hepworth* by Ben Nicholson
● The Tudor Galleries
● *Queen Victoria*, Sir George Hayter
● *The Brontë Sisters*, by Patrick Branwell Brontë
● An unfinished sketch of Jane Austen (c.1810) by her sister, Cassandra

TIP

● Join the Friday Lates for free live music, DJs, talks and events every Friday from 6 to 9pm.

It's always fascinating to see what someone famous looked like and how they chose to be painted. The National Portrait Gallery has iconic images from the Tudors right up to the present day.

British record Founded in 1856 to collect portraits of the great and good in British life, and so inspire others to greatness, this is now the most comprehensive collection of its kind in the world, comprising watercolors, oil paintings, caricatures, silhouettes and photographs.

Start at the top The galleries, incorporating the Ondaatje Wing, are arranged chrono-logically, starting on the second floor—reached by stairs or elevator. Tudor monarchs kick off a visual *Who's Who* of British history that moves

Clockwise from far left: The main entrance to the National Portrait Gallery; the Tudor Galleries; portraits and busts from the Regency period in the Weldon Galleries; an 1834 portrait of the Brontë sisters by their brother, Branwell (right) and Jenny Lind (left)

through inventors, merchants, explorers and empire builders to modern politicians. Here you'll find Isambard Kingdom Brunel, Robert Clive and Warren Hastings of India, Winston Churchill and Margaret Thatcher. There is Chaucer in his floppy hat, Kipling at his desk and A.A. Milne with his engaging tales, Christopher Robin and Winnie-the-Pooh on his knee. Lesser-known sitters also merit a close look, such as the 18th-century portrait of the extensive Sharp family, who formed an orchestra and played at Fulham every Sunday.

Modern times Among the famous portraits from history, you may also spot a number of more familiar, contemporary faces, such as the Duchess of Cambridge, footballer David Beckham, Madonna and J.K. Rowling.

THE BASICS

npg.org.uk

➕ J5

✉ St. Martin's Place, WC2

☎ 020 7306 0055

🕐 Sat–Wed 10–6, Thu–Fri 10–9

🍴 Café, rooftop restaurant

🚇 Leicester Square, Charing Cross

🚉 Charing Cross

♿ Good

💰 Free except for special exhibitions

❓ Lectures, events, apps, explorer touchscreens

HIGHLIGHTS

● Giant Earth sculpture
● Dinosaur skeletons
● Blue whale skeleton
● The Vault, a gallery of crystals, gems and meteorites
● Restless Surface gallery
● Tank room in the Darwin Centre

TIPS

● Use the side entrance on Exhibition Road.
● The museum is huge: plan your visit carefully.

The museum building looks like a Romanesque cathedral and is wittily decorated with a zoo of animals to match its contents—existing animals on the west side, extinct ones on the east side.

Two museums in one Overflowing the British Museum, the Life Galleries were moved here in 1881. They tell the story of life on earth. The story of the Earth itself is told in the Earth Galleries, beginning with a 300-million-year-old fossil of a fern. The Darwin Centre uses technology to make the most of the museum's 70 million objects and make the work of its 300 or so scientists accessible worldwide. Take the glass lift to its futuristic Cocoon building, then wend your way down its sloping walkways, taking in the exciting insect and plant displays.

Clockwise from far left: The Whale Hall; the Red Zone, where galleries explore the nature of the Earth; insect specimens on display at Cocoon, part of the Darwin Centre; the original 1880 Waterhouse Building

Follow the zone The skeleton of a blue whale, the largest creature on Earth, seems to dive through the heart of the great Hintze Hall. This gateway to the galleries was given a spectacular makeover in 2017. Color-coded zones help you plan your visit. In the Red Zone, dramatic sculptures and a giant metallic globe lead to galleries revealing how the planet has evolved and the effects of man on nature. Exhibits in the Green Zone include birds, minerals and creepy crawlies. The Blue Zone celebrates the amazing diversity of our planet, from humans and mammals to fish and dinosaurs. Don't miss the Images of Nature gallery, at the end of the Blue Zone, which houses a stunning collection of art inspired by nature. The superb Darwin Centre and quiet wildlife garden occupy the Orange Zone.

THE BASICS

nhm.ac.uk

➕ B8

✉ Cromwell Road, SW7; also entrance on Exhibition Road

☎ 020 7942 5000

🕐 Daily 10–5.50, last admission 5.30

🍴 Meals, snacks, deli café, picnic areas

🚇 South Kensington

♿ Excellent

✋ Free; charge for some temporary exhibitions

❓ Regular tours, lectures, films, workshops

HIGHLIGHTS

● Springtime daffodils
● Whitehall views from the lake bridge
● Feeding the pelicans, daily 2.30–3
● Views to Buckingham Palace
● Exotic plants in the tropical border

TIPS

● St. James's Café opens early and closes late.
● The park is the perfect setting for summer picnics.
● Cyclists are welcome in the royal parks.

Drop into St. James's Park to picnic and laze on a deckchair, try spotting palaces across the duck-filled lake or follow the Diana, Princess of Wales Memorial Walk.

Royal heart St. James's Park is the oldest and most royal of London's eight royal parks, surrounded by the Palace of Westminster, St. James's Palace, Buckingham Palace and the remains of Whitehall Palace. Kings and their courtiers have been frolicking here since 1532, when Henry VIII laid out a deer park in what was then marshy water meadow and built a hunting lodge that became St. James's Palace. Elizabeth I held fetes here, and in the early 17th century James I began the menagerie, including crocodiles and an elephant that drank a gallon of wine daily.

Left to right: With Buckingham Palace at its western end and the Houses of Parliament within easy reach, the park is a popular retreat for visitors; a drinking fountain; early spring, when the daffodils are in bloom, is one of the best times to visit

French order In the mid-17th century, Charles II, influenced by Versailles, near Paris, redesigned the park to include a canal, Birdcage Walk (where he kept aviaries) and the graveled Mall, where he played pell mell, a game similar to croquet. George IV, helped by John Nash and influenced by Humphrey Repton, softened the formal French lines into the English style in the 19th century, making this 23ha (57-acre) park of blossoming shrubs and curving paths popular with romantics.

Nature As the park is an important migration point and breeding area for birds, two full-time ornithologists look after up to 1,000 birds from more than 45 species. Pelicans live on Duck Island, a tradition begun when the Russian ambassador gave some to Charles II in 1664.

THE BASICS

royalparks.org.uk
J7
The Mall, SW1
0300 061 2350
Daily 5am–midnight
St. James's Café
(▷ 150–151)
St. James's Park, Green Park, Westminster
Victoria
Very good
Free
Changing the Guard (on Horse Guards Parade). Bird talks and guided walks

HIGHLIGHTS

- Sung evensong
- Frescoes and mosaics
- Wren's Great Model in the Triforium (upstairs)
- Triple-layered dome weighing 76,000 tons
- Jean Tijou's wrought-iron sanctuary gates
- Wellington's memorial
- Free organ recitals, Sundays 4.15–5.15
- The view across London
- Wren's tomb and epitaph in the crypt

To slip into St. Paul's for evensong, and sit gazing up at the mosaics as the choir's voices soar, is to enjoy a moment of absolute peace and beauty. At other times, come early or late to avoid the crowds.

Wren's London After the restoration of the monarchy in 1660, artistic patronage bloomed under Charles II. Following the Great Fire of London in 1666, which destroyed four-fifths of the City, Christopher Wren took main stage as King's Surveyor-General. The spires and steeples of his 51 churches, of which 23 still stand, surrounded his masterpiece, St. Paul's.

The fourth St. Paul's This cathedral church for the diocese of London was founded in AD604 by King Ethelbert of Kent. The first three

Clockwise from far left: View of St. Paul's Cathedral from the Millennium Bridge; looking down from the Whispering Gallery; the choir stalls and high altar; St. Paul's before the Great Fire of London in 1666; architect Sir Christopher Wren

The West View of St. Paul's Cathedral before the Fire of London

churches burned down. Wren's, built in stone and paid for with a special coal tax, was the first English cathedral built by a single architect, the only one with a dome, and the only one in the English baroque style. A £40-million cleaning-and-repair project marked the cathedral's 300th anniversary in 2010. Statues and memorials of Britain's famous crowd the interior and crypt—heroes Wellington and Nelson, artists Turner and Reynolds, as well as Wren himself.

The climb The 528 steps to the Golden Gallery at the top of the dome are worth the effort. Shallow steps (237 of them) rise to the Whispering Gallery for views of fine frescoes and colorful 19th-century mosaics. For virtual access to the dome, visit Oculus, a 270-degree film experience in the crypt.

THE BASICS

stpauls.co.uk
✚ N4
✉ Ludgate Hill, EC4
☎ 020 7246 8350
🕐 Mon–Sat 8.30–4.30, last admission 4, Sun for worship only. Daily services range from morning prayer to choral evensong
🍴 Café, tea room
🚇 St. Paul's
🚉 City Thameslink
♿ Very good
💷 Expensive (free entry for worshipers)
❓ Multimedia, audio and guided tours included; organ recitals

If you have ever wondered exactly how a plane flies, how Newton's reflecting telescope worked or how we receive satellite television, you'll find the answers here using interactive exhibits. This is science at its most accessible.

Industry and science Opened in 1857, this museum comes closest to fulfilling Prince Albert's educational aims when he founded the South Kensington Museums after the Great Exhibition of 1851. Its full title is the National Museum of Science and Industry. Over the seven floors, which contain more than 60 collections, the story of human industry, discovery and invention is recounted through various tools and products, from exquisite Georgian cabinets to a satellite launcher.

Clockwise from far left: Chemistry demonstration in the Wonderlab; displays in the Who Am I? gallery explore the wonders of human genetics and intelligence; Handley Page "Gugnunc" airplane from 1929 in Mathematics: The Winton Gallery; the Infinity Boxes exhibit in the Wonderlab

Science made fun See how vital everyday objects were invented and then developed for use in Making the Modern World; find out what makes you smarter than a chimp in Who Am I?; and get involved in the very latest scientific hot topics in Antenna. The galleries vary from rooms of beautiful 18th-century objects to an astronaut's moon capsule and in-depth explanations of abstract concepts. Historic steam engines feature in the Energy Hall, while overhead walkways in the Flight gallery bring you close to some amazing aeroplanes. Discover how mathematics connects to every aspect of our lives in the stunning Zaha Hadid-designed Mathematics: The Winton Gallery, with its flowing, organic shapes, or let the children loose in the high-tech, interactive Wonderlab: The Statoil Gallery.

THE BASICS

sciencemuseum.org.uk

🚲 C8

✉ Exhibition Road, SW7

🕐 Daily 10–6, last admission 5.15 (check website for late opening dates)

🍴 Restaurants, cafés, picnic areas

🚇 South Kensington

♿ Excellent (helpline tel 020 7942 4000)

💵 Free; IMAX and temporary exhibitions expensive; Wonderlab moderate

❓ Guided tours, films, demonstrations, historic characters, workshops

HIGHLIGHTS

- Guided tour storytellers
- Attending a performance
- Interactive displays
- Costume collection

TIP

- Tours and performances take place in all weathers, so dress appropriately.

A faithful reconstruction of the Bard's open-air theater, this South Bank landmark presents many of his plays, as well as work by his contemporaries and new writers.

One man's vision From his first visit to London in 1949, actor and director Sam Wanamaker dreamed of re-creating Shakespeare's 16th-century Globe theater as close as possible to its original site by the Thames at Bankside. Several decades and a long struggle later, the theater opened in 1997 with a production of *Henry V*.

Tradition to the core Constructed of English oak with mortise-and-tenon joints, lime plaster and water-reed thatch roof (the first permitted since the Great Fire of London in 1666), the building techniques used were painstakingly

Left to right: Watching a play at Shakespeare's Globe gives you a unique insight into Elizabethan theater; the Globe has been reconstructed on London's Bankside, a short distance from the site of the original building that hosted Shakespeare's plays

accurate. Its open stage projects into a large circular yard surrounded by three tiers of simple benches (cushions can be hired) for 857 people. Only the seating area and stage are covered, so the 700 "groundlings" standing in the yard below the stage swelter in the heat and get very wet when it rains. An exhibition beneath the theater tells its history and explores the London Shakespeare would have known.

New theater A £7.5-million indoor Jacobean theater, the Sam Wanamaker Playhouse, has created an intimate, year-round theatrical experience, a sharp contrast to the Globe. Performing the plays of Shakespeare and his contemporaries in the surroundings for which they were originally intended, it seats 340 people and is lit by beeswax candles.

THE BASICS

shakespearesglobe.com

🚲 P6

✉ 21 New Globe Walk, SE1

☎ Exhibition and tour office 020 7902 1500; Theatre Box Office 020 7401 9919

🕐 Exhibition daily 9–5; tours daily 9.30–5, every 30 min. Globe performance season mid-Apr to mid-Oct; Sam Wanamaker Playhouse year-round

🍴 Restaurant, bar, café

Ⓜ Blackfriars, Mansion House, London Bridge, Southwark

🚆 London Bridge

🚢 Bankside Pier

♿ Good access; information line tel 020 7902 1409

💷 Expensive (includes guided theater tour and exhibition audio guide)

❓ Temporary exhibitions, full educational schedule

HIGHLIGHTS

- Fountain Court
- Winter ice skating
- Temporary exhibitions
- Free guided tours

Somerset House has been transformed from a historic palace into a riverside arts complex. Spend some time here to enjoy art exhibitions, dancing fountains and summer concerts or festive ice skating.

Palatial home Over the centuries this Thames-side landmark has been home to royalty, the headquarters of the Parliamentary army, stables and apartments, before being demolished in 1775 after decades of neglect. It was rebuilt in 1801 and became the General Register Office, responsible for storing the records of the nation's births, deaths and marriages until 1970. These days, this neoclassical behemoth is used for arts and culture. It's famous for housing the Courtauld Institute of Art in rooms lavishly decorated for the Royal

Clockwise from far left: The courtyard becomes an ice rink in winter; the elegant staircase leading to the upper floors of the Courtauld Gallery; Somerset House lets studios out to artists; the Fountain Courtyard in summer

Academy (▷ 73), before its move to Piccadilly. The Courtauld Gallery owns an impressive collection of works from the early Renaissance to the 20th century (though it is closed for major refurbishment until 2020). A wide variety of events are held here year-round, including London Fashion Week and temporary exhibitions of all kinds.

Courtyard The café-surrounded Edmond J. Safra Fountain Courtyard is an attraction in its own right, with dancing water fountains throughout the summer and open-air film screenings where the audience sits on the cobbles, transforming in December into a spotlit ice rink with a festive feel. The acclaimed Welsh chef Bryn Williams also has a restaurant here (▷ 145).

THE BASICS

somersethouse.org.uk

🔢 L5

✉ Somerset House, Strand, WC2

☎ 020 7845 4600

🕐 Daily 10–6; extended hours for Courtyard, River Terrace and restaurant. Ice rink mid-Nov to mid-Jan

🍽 Cafés, restaurants

🚇 Temple

🚆 Blackfriars, Charing Cross, Waterloo

♿ Excellent

💷 Somerset House free; Courtauld Gallery moderate

❓ Free guided tours of Somerset House Thu 1.15, 2.45, Sat 12.15, 1.15, 2.15 and 3.15. Tickets available from 10.30am at the information desk in the Seamen's Hall, South Wing

HIGHLIGHTS

- The Clore Gallery's huge Turner collection
- *Flatford Mill* by Constable
- *The Opening of Waterloo Bridge* by Constable
- William Hogarth's *Gin Lane* caricature
- Barbara Hepworth's sculptures in stone or wood
- 1960s prints by David Hockney
- Rex Whistler restaurant
- Walk Through British Art chronological displays
- The Tate-to-Tate ferry

With galleries rich in Gainsborough portraits, Turner landscapes, Hepworth sculptures and more, this is an intimate social history of Britain told by its artists.

The Gallery The Tate Gallery was opened in 1897, named after the millionaire Henry Tate, who paid for the core building and donated his Victorian pictures to it. The national collection, renamed Tate Britain after the modern art collection was moved to Tate Modern (▷ 52–53), remains in the original building on Millbank.

The Millbank Project This is a 20-year program of building works designed to transform the gallery. Launched in 2010, the first phase has upgraded the Millbank Entrance, Rotunda and some of the galleries.

Clockwise from far left: The imposing Millbank entrance to Tate Britain; paintings on display in the gallery; the rotunda dome, a masterpiece of Victorian architecture; painting in the Turner Collection, the largest collection of works by J.M.W. Turner in the world, in the modern Clore Gallery

British art The galleries are helpfully divided into four chronological suites. You can follow the visual story of British art from 1500 until the present day. Although paintings, sculptures, installations and works in other media are changed regularly, you may well see van Dyck's lavish portraits of the 17th-century British aristocracy, William Hogarth's prints and richly colored Pre-Raphaelite canvases. Do not miss the great Turner collection housed in the adjoining Clore Gallery.

Turner Prize Britain's most prestigious and controversial prize to celebrate young British talent is run by the Tate and awarded each September. Founded in 1984, winners have included Damien Hirst, Grayson Perry, Duncan Campbell and Chris Ofili.

THE BASICS

tate.org.uk
🚇 J9
✉ Millbank, SW1; entrances on Millbank and Atterbury Street
☎ 020 7887 8888
🕐 Daily 10–6, last admission 5.15
🍴 Restaurant, café
Ⓟ Pimlico, Vauxhall, Westminster
🚆 Vauxhall, Victoria
♿ Very good
🎫 Free; charge for some special exhibitions
❓ Education schedule; Tate app; audio tours

HIGHLIGHTS

● The dramatic Turbine Hall
● Level 9 restaurant
● Installation art
● Interactive digital projects
● The multimedia guides (small charge), Switch House galleries

TIP

● The Tate Boat travels between Tate Modern and Tate Britain every 40 minutes during opening times.

Tate Modern is the most visited modern art gallery in the world, its collection filling the magnificent rejuvenated spaces of George Gilbert Scott's vast Bankside power station.

World-class building Winning an international competition, Swiss architects Herzog & de Meuron were commissioned to convert the brick building. They worked with the size of the power station to create a contemporary gallery space, most notably the majestic Turbine Hall, standing 25m (85ft) from floor to glass-paned ceiling. Notable exhibits here have included Ai Weiwei's *Tree* (2010)—a huge sculpture assembled from dead trees—and Olafur Eliasson's dazzling sun (*The Weather Project*, 2003). Outside, the graceful pedestrian Millennium Bridge spans the Thames.

Clockwise from far left: The monumental Turbine Hall, used for temporary exhibitions; the Millennium Bridge, linking Tate Modern with the City; inside the Switch House extension; The Kiss (1901–04) by Auguste Rodin; Claude Monet's Water Lilies (c.1916)

Artworks Within the spacious galleries, the most influential artists of the 20th century are displayed, including Picasso, Matisse, Dalí, Duchamp, Rodin, Klee and Warhol—as well as British artists such as Bacon, Hepworth, Hockney and Nicholson. Just as much importance is given to performance art, films and installations, many of which you can interact with, down in the Tanks.

Transformation A revitalized gallery opened in 2016. The striking 10-story Switch House extension includes three new levels and a panoramic roof terrace, more than doubling the exhibition space. Accordingly, the gallery's artworks have been completely rehung, showcasing more than 300 artists from around 50 countries.

THE BASICS

tate.org.uk
+ N6
✉ Bankside, SE1
☎ 020 7887 8888
🕐 Sun–Thu 10–6, Fri–Sat 10–10
🍴 Cafés, restaurant
Ⓜ Blackfriars, Southwark
🚆 Blackfriars, London Bridge
♿ Very good
✋ Free; charge for some special exhibitions
❓ Full educational schedule. Choice of free daily guided tours

TOP 25

A cruise along the Thames is a leisurely way to see the city. It gives a new perspective to London's development and history, which is inextricably linked with this great river.

Wonderful sights Many companies run river cruises and water-buses on the Thames. One particularly good stretch is from Westminster Pier in an easterly direction, which takes in a host of sights. This marks the point where the river enters central London and becomes a working highway, until fairly recently lined with shipping, docks and warehouses. At this point the Thames flows between Lambeth Palace and the Houses of Parliament (▷ 22–23) and then past the London Eye (▷ 30–31) and the Southbank Centre, making a northern loop past the Victoria Embankment and toward the

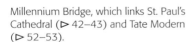

Clockwise from top left: A view over the Thames to St. Paul's Cathedral and the high-rises of the City; tour boat heading up the river towards the City; Big Ben and the Houses of Parliament; the Thames Flood Barrier

Millennium Bridge, which links St. Paul's Cathedral (▷ 42–43) and Tate Modern (▷ 52–53).

Great bridges Beyond the Globe (▷ 46–47) and Southwark Cathedral (▷ 74) the river reaches London Bridge, the modern crossing that replaced the 1831 version, itself replacing its arched medieval predecessor. The next crossing is Tower Bridge (▷ 56–57), designed to allow tall ships passage. On the north bank is the Tower of London (▷ 58–59), placed strategically to protect the port.

Modern versus maritime From here the river passes the redeveloped Docklands. Seafaring is the theme as the Thames reaches Greenwich (▷ 20–21) and then the Thames Barrier.

🕂 K7
✉ Start point: Westminster Pier, SW1
🚇 Westminster
✋ Moderate to expensive
Crown River Cruises
☎ 020 7936 2033, circularcruise.london
City Cruises
☎ 020 7740 0400, citycruises.com
Thames River Services
☎ 020 7930 4097, thamesriverservices.co.uk
Thames Clippers
thamesclippers.com

HIGHLIGHTS

- Bascules being raised
- Glass Floor
- Views from the high-level walkways
- Victorian Engine Rooms
- North Tower exhibition

This iconic bridge over the river is not only a grand feat of engineering, its road bridge still lifting almost daily to allow ships to pass underneath, but also an attraction in its own right.

Construction This great construction project, a bascule and suspension bridge, took hundreds of construction workers more than eight years to complete, opening in 1894. Now powered by electricity, the mechanism used to be steam-driven, and in the Victorian Engine Rooms you step back in time to see the giant coal-driven machines that originally powered the bridge as it opened up to allow huge seafaring vessels to sail underneath. When it was first built, the bridge would be raised at least 20 times a day, and it took more than 80 staff to ensure its

Clockwise from far left: The bridge with the bascules raised; the Glass Floor in the upper walkway; part of the complex machinery in the Engine Rooms

smooth operation. Displays and hands-on mechanisms explore all the different jobs that were needed, from stoker to bridge driver, with real-life stories of former employees.

View from the top You can find out more about the bridge's history and construction in the North Tower exhibition before heading up to the high-level walkways between the North and South towers. From up here you can enjoy the panoramic views of St. Paul's and Canary Wharf, and if you have a head for heights, step out on the Glass Floor, 42m (138ft) above the river, for a bird's-eye view of the road bridge beneath—where the London buses look tiny. If you time it right, this is a spectacular vantage point from which to see the bascules raised (check website for times).

THE BASICS

towerbridge.org.uk

➕ S6

✉ Tower Bridge Road, SE1

☎ 020 7403 3761

🕐 Apr–Sep daily 10–5.30; Oct–Mar daily 9.30–5

🚇 Tower Hill, London Bridge

♿ Good (call ahead of visit to confirm arrangements)

💷 Moderate

HIGHLIGHTS

- Medieval Palace
- Raleigh's room
- Imperial State Crown
- Tower ravens
- Grand Punch Bowl, 1829
- St. John's Chapel

TIPS

- It's cheaper to buy tickets online at hrp.org.uk.
- If buying tickets on the day, it's vital to arrive early.
- Skate the Tower's ice rink (mid-Nov to early Jan).

The superbly restored rooms of Edward I's 13th-century palace bring the Tower alive as the royal palace and place of pageantry it was. Don't miss gazing at the Crown Jewels.

Medieval glory The Tower of London is Britain's best medieval fortress. William the Conqueror (1066–87) began it as a show of brute force and Edward I (1272–1307) completed it. William's Caen stone White Tower, built within old Roman walls, was an excellent defence: It was 27m (90ft) high, with walls 4.5m (15ft) thick, and space for soldiers, servants and nobles. Henry III began the inner wall, the moat, his own water gate—and the royal zoo. Edward I built the outer wall, several towers and Traitor's Gate, and moved the Mint and Crown Jewels here.

Clockwise from far left: The mighty White Tower, begun by William the Conqueror in 1078; Waterloo Block, where the Crown Jewels are on display; historically, Yeoman Warders (known as Beefeaters) are the guardians of the Tower; Tower Green, former scene of private executions

Wonder and horror Stephen (1135–54) was the first king to live here, James I (1603–25) the last. From here Edward I went in procession to his coronation and Henry VIII paraded through the city bedecked in cloth of gold. The Barons seized the Tower to force King John to put his seal to the Magna Carta in 1215, and two princes were murdered while their uncle was being crowned Richard III. Since 1485 it has been guarded by Yeoman Warders or Beefeaters, who also now give guided tours.

Centuries of history The Tower has been a palace, fortress, state prison and execution site and its gates are still locked every night. If the history is overwhelming there is help in the shape of a welcome area, guided tours, an audio tour and numerous interactive displays.

THE BASICS

hrp.org.uk

🞧 S5

✉ Tower Hill, EC3

☎ 020 3166 6000

🕓 Mar–Oct Tue–Sat 9–5.30, Sun–Mon 10–5.30; Nov–Feb Tue–Sat 9–4.30, Sun–Mon 10–4.30

🍴 Cafés, restaurant

🚇 Tower Hill

🚆 Fenchurch Street, London Bridge, Docklands Light Railway (Tower Gateway)

♿ Excellent for Jewel House

🖐 Expensive

❓ Free guided tours every 30 min; audio tours

HIGHLIGHTS

● British Galleries
● Asian collections, with intricate treasures from Afghanistan to ancient India
● Glass collection, from the 13th to 20th centuries
● Leonardo da Vinci notebooks
● Silver Galleries
● The *Hereford Screen* by Sir Gilbert Scott
● The new Exhibition Road Quarter

TIPS

● Enjoy a drink in the Garden or Courtyard cafés.
● Lively events take place on Friday evenings

Part of the V&A's glory is that each room is unexpected—it may contain a French boudoir, plaster casts of classical sculptures, antique silver or contemporary glass.

A vision The V&A started as the South Kensington Museum. It was Prince Albert's vision—arts and science objects available to all people to inspire them to invent and create, with the accent on commercial design and craftsmanship. Since it opened in 1857, its collection, now comprising more than a million works, has become so encyclopedic it ranks as the world's largest decorative arts museum.

Bigger and bigger The existing 11km (7 miles) of gallery space over six floors grew even more impressive with the opening in

Clockwise from left: The V&A, which opened in 1857, now ranks as the world's largest museum of decorative arts; exhibits in the museum's The Renaissance City 1350–1600 display; the Exhibition Road courtyard with its porcelain floor

2017 of a grand new entrance hall and spacious courtyard on Exhibition Road that includes a state-of-the-art subterranean gallery, providing one of the largest temporary exhibition spaces in the UK. The porcelain-tiled courtyard with its glass-fronted café is an exciting venue for installations and events.

Eclectic displays Not every object in the museum is precious, and there are everyday things, unique pieces and opportunities to discover a fascination for a new subject—perhaps lace, ironwork, tiles or Japanese textiles. See the lavishly refurbished Silver Galleries, the magnificent collections in the Medieval and Renaissance galleries, the Raphael Cartoons and the striking Ceramics Gallery and Study Centre.

THE BASICS

vam.ac.uk

➕ C8

✉ Cromwell Road, Exhibition Road, SW7

☎ 020 7942 2000

🕐 Daily 10–5.45 (Fri until 10)

🍴 Restaurant, cafés

🚇 South Kensington

♿ Very good

🎟 Free, except some special exhibitions

❓ Free daily guided, introductory tours. Talks, courses, demonstrations, workshops and concerts

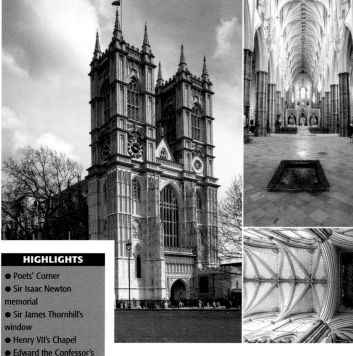

HIGHLIGHTS

- Poets' Corner
- Sir Isaac Newton memorial
- Sir James Thornhill's window
- Henry VII's Chapel
- Edward the Confessor's Chapel
- St. Faith's Chapel
- Grave of the Unknown Soldier
- Little Cloister and College Garden
- Weekday sung evensong at 5pm

TIPS

- Attend a service and hear the choirboys, accompanied by the abbey organ.
- Free organ recitals, Sun 5.45; summer organ festival (mid-Jul to mid-Aug).

The best time to be in the abbey is for the 8am service, sometimes held in St. Faith's Chapel. Follow this with a wander in the nave and cloisters before the crowds arrive.

The kernel of London's second city It was Edward the Confessor who in the 11th century began the rebuilding of the Benedictine abbey church of St. Peter, which was consecrated in 1065. The first sovereign to be crowned there was William the Conqueror in 1066. Successive kings were patrons, as were the pilgrims who flocked to the Confessor's shrine. Henry III (1207–72) employed Master Henry de Reyns to begin the Gothic abbey that stands today, and Henry VII (1457–1509) built his Tudor chapel with its delicate fan vaulting. Since William I, all sovereigns have been crowned

Clockwise from far left: The West Front; the Grave of the Unknown Soldier, adorned with Remembrance Day poppies; the shrine of Edward the Confessor, the abbey's founder; the choir stalls and ornate gilt altar; the abbey's magnificent vaulted ceiling

here—even after Henry VIII broke with Rome in 1533—and all were buried here up to George II (after which Windsor became the royal burial place, ▷ 79). It has also hosted 16 royal marriages, including that of Prince William and Catherine Middleton in 2011.

Daunting riches The abbey is massive, full of monuments, and very popular. From the nave's west end enjoy the view of the abbey, then look over the Victorian Gothic choir screen into Henry V's chantry. Having explored the chapels, the royal necropolis and Poets' Corner, leave time for the quiet cloister with superb views of the flying buttresses supporting the nave. The Queen's Diamond Jubilee Galleries, opened in 2018, are set high up in the medieval triforium, and offer stunning views over the abbey.

THE BASICS

westminster-abbey.org

➕ J8

✉ Broad Sanctuary, SW1; entry by North Door

☎ 020 7222 5152

🕐 Abbey: Mon–Sat times vary, call or check website; no photography. Abbey Museum, College Garden: daily various hours. Closed before special services

🍴 Café

🚇 Westminster, St. James's Park

🚉 Victoria

♿ Good

💷 Expensive

❓ Guided tours, audio guides, app

More to See

This section contains other great places to visit if you have more time. Some are in the heart of the city while others are a short journey away, found under Farther Afield. This chapter also includes fantastic excursions that you should set aside a whole day to visit.

In the Heart of the City

ALBERT MEMORIAL

royalparks.org.uk

George Gilbert Scott's Gothic extravaganza, dedicated to Prince Albert, who died in 1872 at the age of 42, celebrates Victorian achievement with marble statues representing the Arts, Sciences, Industry and Continents. The finely carved frieze at its base depicts famous people in the Arts.

🔆 B7 ✉ Alexandra Gate, Kensington Gardens, SW7 🚇 South Kensington

APSLEY HOUSE (WELLINGTON MUSEUM)

wellingtoncollection.co.uk

The splendid mansion was built for Arthur Wellesley, Duke of Wellington (1769–1852). The sumptuous interior houses his magnificent collection of paintings and decorative arts, with works by Velázquez and Rubens, as well as silver, porcelain and Canova's nude statue of Napoleon.

🔆 F7 ✉ Hyde Park Corner, W1 ☎ 020 7499 5676 🕐 Apr–Oct Wed–Sun 11–5; Nov–Mar Sat–Sun 10–4 🚇 Hyde Park Corner 🎫 Moderate

BANK OF ENGLAND MUSEUM

bankofengland.co.uk/education

Exhibits illustrate the history of Britain's monetary and banking system since 1694. You can see re-creations of Soane's rooms and Sir Herbert Baker's Rotunda.

🔆 Q4 ✉ Bartholomew Lane, EC2 ☎ 020 7601 5545 🕐 Mon–Fri 10–5, last admission 4.30 🚇 Bank 🎫 Free

BANQUETING HOUSE

hrp.org.uk

The only surviving part of the Palace of Whitehall, created by Inigo Jones in 1622, is a spectacular hall with a carved and gilded ceiling, decorated with nine oil paintings by Peter Paul Rubens. Outside is a bust of King Charles I, who was executed here for treason in 1649.

🔆 K6 ✉ Whitehall, SW1 ☎ 020 3166 6155 🕐 Daily 9–5 🚇 Westminster, Charing Cross, Embankment 🎫 Moderate

BOROUGH MARKET

boroughmarket.org.uk

Top-quality produce is offered at London's oldest and most exciting

The glittering Albert Memorial and nearby Royal Albert Hall

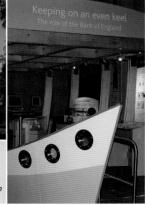

Bank of England Museum

food market, which is very busy on weekends. Many of the traders are artisan producers, keen to share their passion for good food and fine ingredients.

➕ Q6 ✉ Southwark Street, SE1 🕐 Full market Wed–Thu 10–5, Fri 10–6, Sat 8–5; lunch market Mon–Tue 10–5 🚇 London Bridge 🚉 London Bridge

BRITISH LIBRARY
bl.uk

The library is home to well over 150 million items in most known languages, including maps, manuscripts, music scores, patents, sound recordings and eight million stamps. Among its many treasures are a 1215 copy of the Magna Carta, original editions of Chaucer's *Canterbury Tales*, the Gutenberg Bible, Shakespeare's first folio, Handel's *Messiah*, and Leonardo da Vinci's notebook.

➕ J1 ✉ 96 Euston Road, NW1 ☎ 0330 333 1144 🕐 Building Mon–Thu 9.30–8, Fri 9.30–6, Sat 9.30–5, Sun 11–5; check for gallery opening hours 🍴 Café, restaurant 🚇 King's Cross, St Pancras 🎫 Free; charge for special events and exhibitions

CHARLES DICKENS MUSEUM
dickensmuseum.com

Visit the house where Dickens wrote some of his great works, including *Oliver Twist*. You can see Dickens' study, the family bedrooms and servants' quarters, all furnished with many personal items of the Dickens family.

➕ L2 ✉ 48 Doughty Street, WC1 ☎ 020 7405 2127 🕐 Tue–Sun 10–5, last admission 4 🍴 Café 🚇 Russell Square 🎫 Moderate

CHURCHILL WAR ROOMS
iwm.org.uk

Britain's war effort was directed from these secret rooms in a bunker complex beneath Whitehall's streets. The Cabinet War Rooms, where Churchill and his War Cabinet met, offices and dormitories reveal what life was like underground for the hundreds of staff while bombs rained overhead. The Map Room is exactly how it was left when the lights were switched off in August 1945. Interactive displays in the Churchill Museum explore his

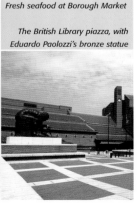

Fresh seafood at Borough Market

The British Library piazza, with Eduardo Paolozzi's bronze statue

fascinating life and legacy with personal letters, extracts from speeches, historic documents, photos and film clips.

⊞ J7 ⊠ Clive Steps, King Charles Street, SW1 ☎ 020 7930 6961 ⏰ Daily 9.30–6 🍴 Café 🚇 St. James's Park, Westminster 💷 Expensive

CITY HALL
london.gov.uk
Sir Norman Foster's distinctive glass building on the Thames is the office of the Mayor of London and the capital's governing body, the London Assembly. The Scoop, an outdoor amphitheater, seats 800 for summer events.

⊞ R6 ⊠ The Queen's Walk, SE1 ☎ 020 7983 4100 ⏰ Mon–Thu 8.30–6, Fri 8.30–5.30 🚇 London Bridge 💷 Free

CLARENCE HOUSE
royalcollection.org.uk
Built for Prince William, Duke of Clarence and later William IV, this has been renovated by its current resident, the Prince of Wales. Five rooms used by Prince Charles and his wife, the Duchess of Cornwall,

can be seen, in August only. Booking is essential.

⊞ H7 ⊠ Off the Mall, SW1 ☎ 020 7766 7303 ⏰ Guided tours Aug Mon–Fri 10–4.30, Sat–Sun 10–5.30 🚇 St. James's Park, Green Park 💷 Expensive

CLEOPATRA'S NEEDLE
Far older than Cleopatra, this impressive 26m (86ft) pink granite obelisk was constructed in Ancient Egypt in 1450BC and records the triumphs of Rameses the Great.

⊞ K6 ⊠ Victoria Embankment, WC2 🚇 Embankment, Charing Cross 💷 Free

DESIGN MUSEUM
designmuseum.org
Devoted to contemporary design and architecture, with three galleries under a suitably spectacular roof, the museum tells the story of design and its impact on our lives.

⊞ Off map at A7 ⊠ 224–238 Kensington High Street, W8 ☎ 020 3862 5900 ⏰ Daily 10–6 🍴 Restaurant, café 🚇 Kensington High Street, Holland Park 💷 Free; temporary exhibitions expensive

City Hall, home to the London Assembly

EROS STATUE

Alfred Gilbert's iconic memorial (1893) to the philanthropic 7th Earl of Shaftesbury (1801–85), *The Angel of Christian Charity*, is popularly referred to as Eros, although it actually depicts his twin brother, Anteros, the god of selfless love.

➕ H5 ✉ Piccadilly Circus, W1
🚇 Piccadilly Circus

FOUNDLING MUSEUM

foundlingmuseum.org.uk

When Thomas Coram founded a hospice for abandoned children in 1739, Handel and Hogarth helped to raise funds. Both the 1930s building and the art, which includes works by Gainsborough, Hogarth and Millais, are magnificent. The collection has everyday items that were used in the Foundling Hospital and recordings of moving oral testimonies from former residents.

➕ K2 ✉ 40 Brunswick Square, WC1
☎ 020 7841 3600 🕐 Tue–Sat 10–5,
Sun 11–5 🍽 Café 🚇 Russell Square
♿ Moderate

GARDEN MUSEUM

gardenmuseum.org.uk

Celebrating the plant-hunting Tradescant family and 400 years of British garden and plant history in an old church, knot garden and gallery, the Garden Museum was given a £7.5 million transformation in 2017.

➕ L8 ✉ Lambeth Palace Road, SE1
☎ 020 7401 8865 🕐 Sun–Fri 10.30–5,
Sat 10.30–4; closed 1st Mon each month
🍽 Café 🚇 Lambeth North ♿ Moderate

THE GHERKIN

thegherkinlondon.com

This dazzling 21st-century tower, officially No. 30 St. Mary Axe, adds wit to the cluster of tall buildings in London's financial hub.

➕ R4 ✉ 30 St. Mary Axe, EC3 🕐 Not
open to the general public 🚇 Bank

GOLDEN HINDE II

goldenhinde.co.uk

The ship is an exact replica of the 16th-century galleon in which Sir Francis Drake circumnavigated the globe, and hosts regular family events and costumed tours.

Design Museum interior

Eros, at the heart of Piccadilly Circus

🚇 Q6 ✉ St. Mary Overie Dock, Cathedral Street, SE1 ☎ 020 7403 0123 🕐 Apr–Oct daily 10–6; Nov–Mar daily 10–5
🍴 Refreshment kiosks 🚇 London Bridge
🚉 London Bridge 💰 Moderate

GREEN PARK

royalparks.org.uk

Covering 19ha (47 acres), Green Park is a popular venue for picnics, and famous for its mature oak and birch trees lining the avenues, grass lawns and attractive spring daffodil displays. Striped deckchairs are available to rent.

🚇 G7 ✉ SW1 ☎ 0300 061 2350
🕐 Daily 5am–midnight 🚇 Green Park, Hyde Park Corner 💰 Free

GUILDHALL ART GALLERY

cityoflondon.gov.uk

The intriguing gallery displays a quirky collection of mostly British artwork, plus part of Roman London's huge amphitheater, built in AD200 and discovered in 1985.

🚇 P4 ✉ Guildhall Yard, Gresham Street, EC2 ☎ 020 7332 3700 🕐 Mon–Sat 10–5, Sun 12–4 🚇 St. Paul's, Bank 💰 Free; charge for some temporary exhibitions

HANDEL & HENDRIX IN LONDON

handelhendrix.org

Handel's house is at 25 Brook Street, and Jimi Hendrix's flat is on the top floor of 23. The first was home to the composer of *The Messiah* from 1723 to 1759, while the second was where the American guitarist, singer and songwriter lived for a short time between 1968 and 1969. Displays, talks and events celebrate these contrasting musicians, including regular baroque recitals.

🚇 G5 ✉ 25 and 23 Brook Street, W1
☎ 020 7495 1685 🕐 Mon–Sat 11–6
🚇 Bond Street, Oxford Circus
💰 Moderate

HMS *BELFAST*

iwm.org.uk

Clamber around this 1938 war cruiser, visiting the cabins, gun tur- rets, dining hall, bridge and boiler room to get a taste of life on board a warship. Real-life accounts of some of the 950-strong crew to bring it all to life.

The retired 1938 war cruiser HMS Belfast

➕ R6 ✉ The Queen's Walk, SE1 ☎ 020
7940 6300 🕒 Daily 10–6 🍴 Café
🚇 London Bridge 🚉 London Bridge
💷 Expensive

HOLY TRINITY, SLOANE SQUARE

holytrinitysloanesquare.co.uk
London's best Arts and Crafts
church has glass by Burne-Jones
and William Morris. Note the huge
east window with its 48 panels
depicting saints.
➕ E9 ✉ Sloane Square, SW1 ☎ 020
7730 7270 🕒 Daily 9–5 🚇 Sloane Square
💷 Donation

HYDE PARK

royalparks.org.uk
One of the city's largest open
spaces, the park was tamed in the
18th century and is the perfect
place for a leisurely picnic. Don't
miss the views from the
Serpentine Bridge, the Rose
Garden or the Diana Fountain.
➕ E6 ✉ W2 ☎ 0300 061 2114 🕒 Daily
5am–midnight 🍴 Restaurant, café
🚇 Hyde Park Corner, Knightsbridge,
Lancaster Gate 💷 Free

LEADENHALL BUILDING

theleadenhallbuilding.com
The stunning 224m (734ft) glass
and steel "Cheesegrater", in the
heart of the financial district, was
designed by Richard Rogers.
➕ R4 ✉ 122 Leadenhall Street, EC3
🕒 Limited public access 🚇 Bank

LONDON MITHRAEUM

www.londonmithraeum.com
This multi-sensory museum
about the Roman Temple of
Mithras displays objects discovered
when the site was excavated.
➕ P5 ✉ 12 Walbrook, EC4 🕒 Tue–Sat
10–6, Sun 12–5 🚇 Bank, St. Paul's,
Mansion House 💷 Free

LONDON TRANSPORT MUSEUM

ltmuseum.co.uk
With beautifully restored old red
double-decker buses, trams,
trolleybuses and Tube trains,
themed galleries tell the story of
London's transportation system.
➕ K5 ✉ Covent Garden Piazza, WC2
☎ 020 7379 6344 🕒 Daily 10–6 🍴 Café
🚇 Covent Garden 🚉 Charing Cross
💷 Expensive

The Diana, Princess of Wales Memorial Fountain, Hyde Park

MADAME TUSSAUDS

madametussauds.com

See how many famous people you can identify, from Shakespeare to Donald Trump, or be a judge on singing talent show *The Voice* and immerse yourself in the *Star Wars* exhibition. It gets very crowded in peak holiday times.

🔛 E3 ✉ Marylebone Road, NW1 ☎ 0333 321 2001 🕐 Check website 🍴 Café 🚇 Baker Street 💷 Expensive; family ticket available

PETER PAN STATUE

George Frampton's bronze statue (1912) commemorating J.M. Barrie's fictional creation Peter Pan, the boy who never grew up, stands in Kensingston Gardens, west of the Long Water.

🔛 B6 ✉ Long Water, Kensington Gardens, W2 🚇 Lancaster Gate

PETRIE MUSEUM

ucl.ac.uk/culture/petrie-museum

The ancient spoils of many Egyptologists' explorations are on display at the tucked-away Petrie Museum of Egyptian Archaeology. With 80,000 objects, it's one of the world's greatest collections of Egyptian and Sudanese archaeology.

🔛 J2 ✉ University College London, Malet Place, WC1 ☎ 020 7679 2884 🕐 Tue–Sat 1–5 🚇 Euston Square 💷 Free

PHOTOGRAPHERS' GALLERY

thephotographersgallery.org.uk

An Edwardian warehouse has been transformed into a state-of-the-art home for the gallery, with three floors of exhibition space, a bookshop and café. It also hosts a range of talks and events.

🔛 H4 ✉ 16–18 Ramillies Street, W1 ☎ 020 7087 9300 🕐 Mon–Sat 10–6, Thu until 8 during exhibitions, Sun 11–6 🚇 Oxford Circus 💷 Inexpensive; free Mon–Fri 10–12 and for under 16s

POSTAL MUSEUM

postalmuseum.org

Packed with surprises and interest, this modern museum tells the story of communication by post since Victorian times and includes an exciting 15-minute subterranean ride on the Mail Rail.

Postal Museum underground tour

Wax figures at Madame Tussauds

⊞ L2 ✉ 15–20 Phoenix Place, WC1
☎ 0300 030 0700 ◷ Daily 10–5 🍴 Café
Ⓜ Farringdon, Russell Square 💰 Expensive

REGENT'S PARK

royalparks.org.uk

Enjoy the vast rose gardens (with 12,000 roses), boating lake, sports facilities, playgrounds, London Zoo (▷ 75) and the open-air theater from May to September. There's also a large wetland area, home to 100 species of wild bird. Adjacent Primrose Hill boasts famous views over the city.

⊞ D1–F2 ✉ Regent's Park, NW1 ☎ 0300 061 2300 ◷ Daily from 5am. Closing times change seasonally 🍴 Cafés Ⓜ Regent's Park, Camden Town 💰 Free

ROYAL ACADEMY OF ARTS

royalacademy.org.uk

The RA hosts major art shows, plus the annual Summer Exhibition, held every year since 1769. A major redevelopment opened up new areas to celebrate its 250th anniversary in 2018, linking Burlington House and Burlington Gardens for the first time.

⊞ H5 ✉ Burlington House, Piccadilly, W1
☎ 020 7300 8090 ◷ Daily 10–6, Fri until 10 🍴 Restaurant, café Ⓜ Green Park, Piccadilly Circus 💰 Free; temporary exhibitions expensive

ST. JAMES'S, PICCADILLY

sjp.org.uk

Wren's church (1682–84), built for the local aristocracy, has a sumptuous interior. Some superb concerts are held here, and the courtyard hosts market stalls.

⊞ H6 ✉ 197 Piccadilly, W1 ☎ 020 7734 4511 ◷ Check website 🍴 Café
Ⓜ Piccadilly Circus 💰 Donation

ST. KATHARINE DOCKS

skdocks.co.uk

Luxury yachts now fill the marina close to Tower Bridge where cargoes were once landed, while restaurants, shops and apartments fill the former warehouses. Explore the World Food Market at Marble Quay on Saturdays, from 11 to 3.

⊞ S6 ✉ St. Katharine's Way, E1 ☎ 020 7264 5287 Ⓜ Tower Hill 🚆 Tower Gateway (DLR), Fenchurch Street 🚢 Tower Pier, St. Katharine's Pier 💰 Free

MORE TO SEE

The Royal Academy of Arts

SEA LIFE LONDON AQUARIUM

visitsealife.com/london

More than 3,000 forms of marine life, including sharks, stingrays and turtles, fill this aquatic spectacular. Stroke a crab in the rock pool exhibit or catch a piranha feeding frenzy in the rainforest section. You can also book to dive with sharks (extra cost).

➕ L7 ✉ County Hall, SE1 🕐 Mon–Fri 10–6, Sat–Sun 10–7 🚇 Westminster, Waterloo 💷 Expensive

SIR JOHN SOANE'S MUSEUM

soane.org

The gloriously overfurnished home of neoclassical architect and avid collector Sir John Soane (1753–1837) is full of surprises. Canaletto's paintings hang in the breakfast room, Hogarth's *Rake's Progress* unfolds from the walls, and there's an Egyptian pharaoh's sarcophagus downstairs. It's all too easy to miss a Watteau drawing or a rare Etruscan vase.

➕ L4 ✉ 13 Lincoln's Inn Fields, WC2 ☎ 020 7405 2107 🕐 Wed–Sun 10–5 🚇 London Bridge 🚉 Holborn 💷 Free

SOUTHWARK CATHEDRAL

cathedral.southwark.anglican.org

The imposing stone building is reflective of its medieval origins, despite much rebuilding over the centuries. Inside, there are choir stalls and interesting monuments.

➕ Q6 ✉ London Bridge, SE1 ☎ 020 7367 6700 🕐 Mon–Fri 8–6, Sat–Sun 8.30–6 🍴 Café 🚇 London Bridge 🚉 London Bridge 💷 Donation

SPENCER HOUSE

spencerhouse.co.uk

This lavishly restored Palladian mansion is a rare survivor of 18th-century aristocratic St. James's and Mayfair. Explore eight rooms with gilded decorations, period paintings and furniture, along with the restored garden.

➕ H6 ✉ 27 St. James's Place, SW1 ☎ 020 7514 1958 🕐 Sun from 10.30 (last tour 4.30). Closed Aug. Guided tours only 🚇 Green Park 💷 Expensive; no children under 10

TRAFALGAR SQUARE

Sir Edwin Landseer's lions protect Nelson's Column, erected to

Southwark Cathedral retains a medieval appearance despite much rebuilding

The Picture Room in Sir John Soane's Museum

commemorate the 1805 Battle of Trafalgar, at the heart of this iconic square. The fountains were added in 1845. Bronze statues occupy three of the plinths; the fourth hosts changing works by contemporary artists.

✚ J6 🚇 Charing Cross 🚆 Charing Cross 🎫 Free

THE VIEW FROM THE SHARD

theviewfromtheshard.com

Occupying floors 68–72 of the Shard, London's (indeed, Western Europe's) tallest landmark at 310m (1,016ft), the viewing galleries offer 360-degree panoramas across the city and beyond. Regular events include yoga and pilates classes and silent discos.

✚ Q6 ✉ Joiner Street, SE1 ☎ 0344 499 7222 🕙 Sun–Wed 10–8, Thu–Sat 10–10 🚇 London Bridge 🚆 London Bridge 🎫 Expensive

WALLACE COLLECTION

wallacecollection.org

Works by Velázquez, Titian, Rubens and Rembrandt and exquisite French furniture, Sèvres porcelain and a spectacular array of princely arms and armor are elegantly displayed in a historic London town house. Its notable restaurant is located in the glass-roofed courtyard.

✚ F4 ✉ Hertford House, Manchester Square, W1 ☎ 020 7563 9500 🕙 Daily 10–5 🍽 Restaurant, café 🚇 Marble Arch, Bond Street 🎫 Free

ZSL LONDON ZOO

zsl.org

More than 750 species call London Zoo home and, from the penguin beach to the Gorilla Kingdom and Indian-themed Land of the Lions, their accommodations are impressive. With walk-through enclosures (inlcuding Europe's only spider walk-through!), diverse environments, daily demonstrations, talks and feeds, the zoo makes a great family day out.

✚ Off map at G1 ✉ Outer Circle, Regents Park, NW1 ☎ 0344 225 1826 🕙 Daily from 10; closing times vary 🍽 Restaurants, cafés 🚇 Regents Park, Camden Town 🎫 Expensive

Bustling Trafalgar Square, a popular meeting place

Farther Afield

CANARY WHARF

canarywharf.com

Scintillating modern architecture dominates this premier business, shopping and leisure district built on former docklands.

⊞ See map ▷ 115　✉ Canary Wharf, E14　☎ 020 7477 1477　⊙ Individual shops, bars and restaurants differ　🚇 Canary Wharf

CHELSEA PHYSIC GARDEN

chelseaphysicgarden.co.uk

One of London's hidden gems, this walled garden was founded in 1673 to train apothecaries' apprentices in the identification of medicinal plants.

⊞ See map ▷ 114　✉ 66 Royal Hospital Road, SW3　☎ 020 7352 5646　⊙ Sun–Fri; opening times vary　🍴 Café　🚇 Sloane Square　💷 Expensive

CHISWICK HOUSE

chiswickhouseandgardens.org.uk

Lord Burlington's exquisite country villa (1725–29), inspired by the architecture of classical Italy, has superb formal gardens.

⊞ See map ▷ 114　✉ Burlington Lane, W4　☎ 020 3141 3350　⊙ House: Apr–Oct

Wed–Mon 10–5. Garden: daily 7–dusk　🍴 Café　🚇 Turnham Green　🚉 Chiswick　💷 House: moderate. Garden: free

DULWICH PICTURE GALLERY

dulwichpicturegallery.org.uk

Opened in 1814 as England's first purpose-built public art gallery, this attractive venue is home to a fabulous collection of old masters.

⊞ See map ▷ 115　✉ Gallery Road, SE21　☎ 020 8693 5254　⊙ Tue–Sun 10–5　🍴 Café　🚉 North or West Dulwich　💷 Moderate

HAM HOUSE AND GARDEN

nationaltrust.org.uk

Immerse yourself in the 17th century in this stately home, with its valuable furnishings, summer houses and kitchen gardens.

⊞ See map ▷ 114　✉ Ham, Richmond, Surrey, TW10　☎ 020 8940 1950　⊙ Check website or phone for details　🍴 Café　🚇 Richmond, then bus 371　💷 Expensive

HAMPSTEAD HEATH

cityoflondon.gov.uk

Hampstead Heath offers 325ha (800 acres) of open countryside

Historic Ham House and gardens, built in 1610 on the banks of the Thames

The Museum of London Docklands

to enjoy in north London, including a zoo and a lido.

➕ See map ▷ 114 ✉ Hampstead, NW3
☎ 020 7482 7073 for visitor information
Ⓜ Hampstead 🖐 Free

HIGHGATE CEMETERY

highgatecemetery.org

The resting place of countless luminaries from Karl Marx to Malcolm McLaren, this vast, prestigious cemetery opened in 1839 and is a tranquil spot to explore. Split over two sites, there are guided tours available (essential for entry to West Cemetery).

➕ See map ▷ 114 ✉ Swain's Lane, N6
☎ 020 8340 1834 🕐 Mar–Oct daily 10–5; Nov–Feb daily 10–4 Ⓜ Archway 🖐 East Cemetery inexpensive; West Cemetery expensive

JEWISH MUSEUM

jewishmuseum.org.uk

This vibrant museum explores the history of Jewish people in Britain, and includes the powerful Holocaust Gallery.

➕ See map ▷ 114 ✉ 129–131 Albert Street, NW1 ☎ 020 7284 7384 🕐 Sat–Thu 10–5, Fri 10–2 🍴 Kosher café Ⓜ Camden Town 🖐 Moderate

KENWOOD

english-heritage.org.uk

Restyled by Robert Adam, this country house with landscaped parkland lies outside pretty Hampstead village. Its walls are hung with Rembrandts, Romneys, Vermeers and Gainsboroughs. In summer, evening concerts are held in the grounds.

➕ See map ▷ 114 ✉ Hampstead Lane, NW3 ☎ 020 8348 1286 🕐 Apr–Oct daily 10–5; Nov–Mar daily 10–4 🍴 Café Ⓜ Hampstead Heath 🖐 Free

KEW GARDENS

kew.org

With 44,000 plants and some glorious glasshouses, the 120ha (300-acre) Royal Botanic Garden at Kew is a magical place. Pleasant tree-shaded avenues, seasonal flower displays, a treetop walkway, a multi-sensory giant beehive and Kew Palace and its Royal Kitchens are just some of the attractions.

➕ See map ▷ 114 ✉ Richmond, TW9
☎ 020 8332 5655 🕐 Daily from 10; closing times vary 🍴 Café Ⓜ Kew Gardens
Ⓡ Richmond, then bus 65 🖐 Expensive

MUSEUM OF LONDON DOCKLANDS

museumoflondon.org.uk/docklands

The museum tells the story of London's river, port and people from Roman times until now.

➕ See map ▷ 115 ✉ No. 1 Warehouse, West India Quay, E14 ☎ 020 7001 9844
🕐 Daily 10–6 🍴 Restaurant, café Ⓜ West India Quay, Canary Wharf 🖐 Free

PORTOBELLO ROAD MARKET

portobelloroad.co.uk

Famed for its antiques, Portobello Road also hosts a series of markets where everything imaginable is sold. Saturday is the biggest day.

➕ See map ▷ 114 ✉ Portobello Road, W11 🕐 Mon–Wed 9–6, Thu 9–1, Fri–Sat 9–7 Ⓜ Ladbroke Grove, Notting Hill Gate

V&A MUSEUM OF CHILDHOOD

vam.ac.uk/moc

Exhibits here explore playtime from 1600 to the present day, with Noah's arks, dolls, toy soldiers, games and mechanical toys.

➕ See map ▷ 115 ✉ Cambridge Heath Road, E2 ☎ 020 8983 5200 🕐 Daily 10–5.45 🍴 Café Ⓜ Bethnal Green
Ⓡ Bethnal Green 🖐 Free

Excursions

HAMPTON COURT PALACE

hrp.org.uk

When King Henry VIII dismissed his chancellor, Cardinal Wolsey, in 1529, he took over Wolsey's already ostentatious Tudor palace and enlarged it. Successive monarchs altered and repaired both the palace and its 24ha (60 acres) of beautiful Tudor and baroque gardens.

The best way to visit this huge collection of chambers, courtyards and state apartments is to follow one of the six clearly indicated routes. Highlights include Henry VIII's Great Hall, which is recognized as England's finest medieval hall; the Chapel Royal, still in use after 450 years; and the vast Tudor kitchens, built to feed Henry VIII's court, providing more than 600 meals twice a day. Allow at least three hours for your visit, ending with the formal Tudor gardens that reach down to the River Thames, the famous maze and restored Privy Garden.

Children love Hampton Court, not least because there are so many events and activities designed especially for them, including costumed presentations and family audio guides and trails.

Distance: 22.5km (14 miles)

Journey time: 35 min

✉ East Molesey, Surrey, KT8 ☎ 020 3166 6000 🕐 Apr–Oct daily 10–6; Nov–Mar 10–4.30 🍴 Café, restaurant 🚇 Waterloo to Hampton Court 🚢 Riverboat to Hampton Court 💷 Expensive

WARNER BROS. STUDIO TOUR LONDON—THE MAKING OF HARRY POTTER™

wbstudiotour.co.uk

Once *Harry Potter and the Deathly Hallows* wrapped in 2010, all the custom-made artifacts, costumes and iconic sets were preserved and can now be seen on a site adjacent to the studios where all eight Potter films were made.

Sets to explore include the Great Hall, with hand-crafted props and Hogwarts costumes; Platform 9¾ and the Hogwarts Express; the Forbidden Forest, complete with animatronic spiders; and Diagon Alley, home of Ollivanders wand

The elegant formal flower gardens at Hampton Court Palace

Model of Hogwarts at Harry Potter Studios

shop. A highlight is the spectacular model of Hogwarts Castle, an intricate work of art whose every courtyard, turret and tower were filmed and then digitally enhanced to use in the films.

You can also don a robe and fly on a broomstick, ride on the Hogwarts Express or sample a glass of butterbeer in the café.

Distance: 32km (20 miles)
Journey time: 40 min
✉ Studio Tour Drive, Leavesden, WD25
☎ 0345 084 0900 ☻ Daily 9am–10pm (entry by timed slot; advance booking essential) 🍴 Café 🚇 Euston to Watford Junction, then shuttle bus 💷 Expensive

WINDSOR CASTLE

royalcollection.org.uk
Fairy-tale towers and turrets make this the ultimate royal castle. An official residence of Her Majesty the Queen, it's the oldest and largest occupied castle in the world.

Begun by William the Conqueror and rebuilt in stone by Henry II, the castle has been embellished over the centuries. The richly decorated State Apartments are hung with old masters, including works by Rembrandt, Rubens and Canaletto. The tombs of 10 sovereigns, including Henry VIII and Charles I, lie in fine Gothic St. George's Chapel, a popular venue for royal weddings—both Prince Harry and Princess Eugenie got married here in 2018.

Should the State Apartments or chapel be closed, there is still much to see. The Drawings Gallery has changing exhibitions, and don't miss Queen Mary's Dolls' House, designed by Edward Lutyens. Some 1,500 craftspeople were involved in its construction.

A colorful spectacle, Changing the Guard usually takes place at 11am within the castle grounds on Mondays, Wednesdays, Fridays and Saturdays, weather permitting.

Distance: 40km (25 miles)
Journey time: 40–55 min
✉ Windsor, Berkshire, SL4 ☎ 0303 123 7304 ☻ Mar–Oct daily 10–5.15; Nov–Feb daily 10–4.15 🚇 Waterloo to Windsor & Eton Riverside, Paddington to Windsor & Eton Central 💷 Expensive (includes audio tour)

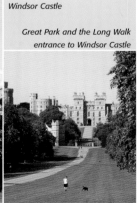

Windsor Castle

Great Park and the Long Walk entrance to Windsor Castle

City Tours

This section contains self-guided tours that will help you explore the sights in each of the city's regions. Each tour is designed to take a day, with a map pinpointing the recommended places along the way. There is a quick reference guide at the end of each tour, listing everything you need in that region, so you know exactly what's close by.

CITY TOURS

South Bank

With sweeping river views, exciting contemporary art at Tate Modern, medieval history at Southwark Cathedral, world-class concert halls and a theatrical tradition dating back to Shakespeare's time, the South Bank has plenty to entice visitors.

Morning

Start at **Tower Bridge** and set the scene for your day with high-level, panoramic views, spotting London's tallest landmark, the **Shard** (▷ 75). Then stroll among the converted warehouses of Shad Thames, home to numerous shops and cafés. Join the well-signed riverside Thames Path, passing the distinctive **City Hall** (▷ 68), seat of London's government, and the moored war cruiser **HMS** *Belfast* (right, ▷ 70).

Mid-morning

From Tooley Street, zigzag under **London Bridge** to visit **Southwark Cathedral** (left, ▷ 74). Admire the soaring nave, choir and 16th-century Great Screen, and look for stained-glass windows depicting famous Southwark inhabitants, including Chaucer and Shakespeare. The **Harvard Chapel** reveals some of the cathedral's many links with America.

Lunch

Borough Market (right, ▷ 66–67) is nearby and the perfect location for lunch, especially Wednesdays to Saturdays when it's packed with enticing food stalls and the restaurants are particularly lively.

Afternoon

Return to the riverside, passing the fine 14th-century rose window in the ruins of **Winchester Palace**, to see the replica of Sir Francis Drake's magnificent galleon, *Golden Hinde II* (right, ▷ 69–70). Walk through medieval Clink Street, once the site of a notorious prison, now a museum. Pass under Southwark Bridge. Restaurants, cafés and pubs with river views line the route to **Shakespeare's Globe** (▷ 46–47), a faithful reconstruction of an Elizabethan open-air theater. Don't miss its guided tours.

Mid-afternoon

Explore the contemporary art at **Tate Modern** (▷ 52–53) and take time for tea in its café with a view. Continue your stroll along the Thames Path, enjoying views of the architecture lining the opposite bank of the river. Have a look in the crafts studios on the lower floors of the **Oxo Tower** (left) and in nearby **Gabriel's Wharf**, before you reach **Waterloo Bridge**—you may find a secondhand books market under its arches—and the **Southbank Centre**.

Dinner

There's a vast choice of restaurants around here, but if you're up for somewhere smart with unmatched views, book a table at the **Oxo Tower Bar, Brasserie and Restaurant** (▷ 149).

Evening

With concerts by world-class musicians at the **Royal Festival Hall** (▷ 138), plays at the **National Theatre** (▷ 136) and films at **BFI Southbank** (▷ 133), you're spoiled for choice for entertainment in this part of London. Free live music events are often held in the early evening. A ride on the **London Eye** (right, ▷ 30–31) at night is a magical experience.

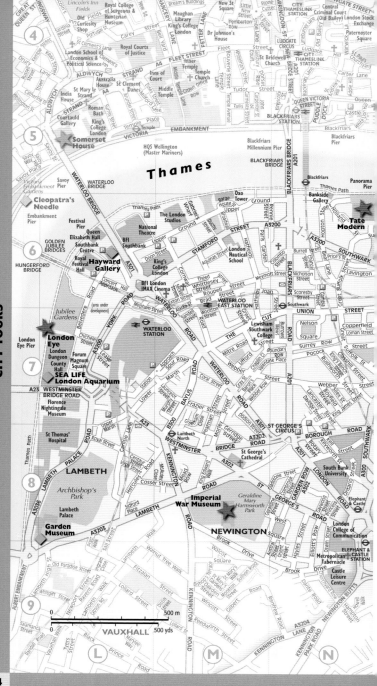

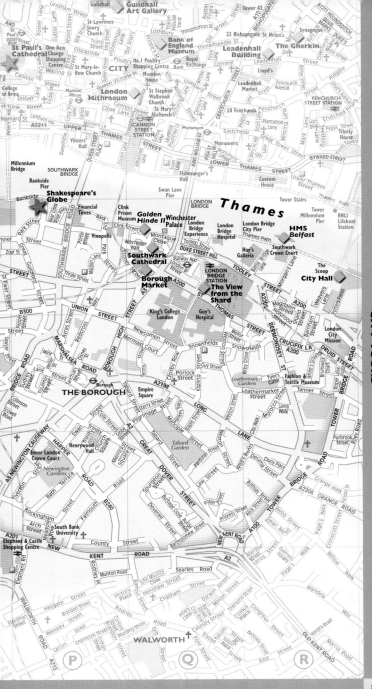

South Bank Quick Reference Guide

Imperial War Museum (▷ 24)
The First World War galleries are a highlight in this museum, focusing on the social impact of warfare through film, painting and sound archives. Discover the stories behind the dramatic Witnesses to War displays in the soaring atrium.

London Eye (▷ 30)
On a clear day you can see 40km (25 miles) from the top, across London and as far as Windsor Castle (▷ 79). With four million people stepping on board every year to enjoy the bird's-eye views, it is Britain's most popular paid tourist attraction.

Shakespeare's Globe (▷ 46)
Shakespeare's Globe was built as a result of the passionate vision of Sam Wanamaker. As well as a faithful reconstruction of the Bard's open-air theater, the site also includes a smaller, candlelit playhouse named after the American actor who created this impressive South Bank landmark.

Tate Modern (▷ 52)
At the foot of the Millennium Bridge and presenting a distinctive face to the Thames, Tate Modern welcomes nearly five million visitors each year. The building itself, a converted power station, is almost as fascinating as the art.

Golden Hinde II

Fleet Street to the Tower

On this tour, see where the Romans founded Londinium in the first century AD and discover the city's long and fascinating history through its architecture, from Sir Christopher Wren's magnificent churches to the great Tower of London, with stories to capture everyone's imagination.

Morning
Arrive early at **St. Paul's Cathedral** (right, ▷ 42–43) before the crowds descend to fully appreciate its magnificence. The cathedral opens for sightseeing at 8.30am, but there are services, usually at 7.30am and 8am, which you could attend. Pâtisserie **Paul** (▷ 126) in Paternoster Square is the perfect place to stop for a snack.

Mid-morning
Walk up St. Martin's Aldersgate to the **Museum of London** (left, ▷ 32–33) and spend some time exploring its immense collection. Retracing your steps, turn left into Gresham Street. Ahead is **St. Lawrence Jewry** church, with dark wooden pews and a gold-encrusted ceiling lit by chandeliers. Cross the Guildhall Yard to visit the **Guildhall Art Gallery** (▷ 70).

Lunch
Walk down King Street and turn right into Cheapside for an early lunch at Café Below in the crypt of **St. Mary-le-Bow**, a Wren church with striking modern stained-glass windows. A statue of Captain John Smith (1580–1631), leader of the Virginia Colony at Jamestown, presides over the square.

Afternoon

After lunch, turn down Bow Churchyard passage, then turn right into Bow Lane, lined with smart shops and eateries, to cross Watling Street. On the left is the **Guild Church of St. Mary Aldermary**. It's worth stepping inside to admire the magnificent ceiling.

The ruins of the Temple of Mithras, preserved in the **London Mithraeum** (▷ 71), stand amid the soaring glass-and-steel modernity of the City's financial institutions. Ahead you'll see the distinctive **Gherkin** (▷ 69), officially No. 30 St. Mary Axe. Passing the great pillars of the Mansion House, with the Bank of England in view, window-shop in the **Royal Exchange** (right, ▷ 126) before exploring the food stands in **Leadenhall Market** (▷ 126).

Mid-afternoon

Head down Philpot Lane to the Thames, pausing to admire Wren's towering **Monument** (to the Great Fire of London) on your right; you can climb this for spectacular views. The riverside walkway past Customs House leads you to the **Tower of London** (below, ▷ 58–59). Aim to arrive by 2pm. First, take a tour with one of the Yeoman Warders, then spend the rest of the afternoon soaking up the history.

Evening

Sit by the Thames and enjoy the views of **Tower Bridge** (▷ 56–57) and the south bank of the river. Walk through to **St. Katharine Docks** (▷ 73–74) and stroll among the smart yachts in the marina. The renovated warehouses there house a host of bars and restaurants in which to relax. Alternatively, take the Circle Line tube from Tower Hill to Farringdon for a gastropub experience at **The Peasant** (▷ 149).

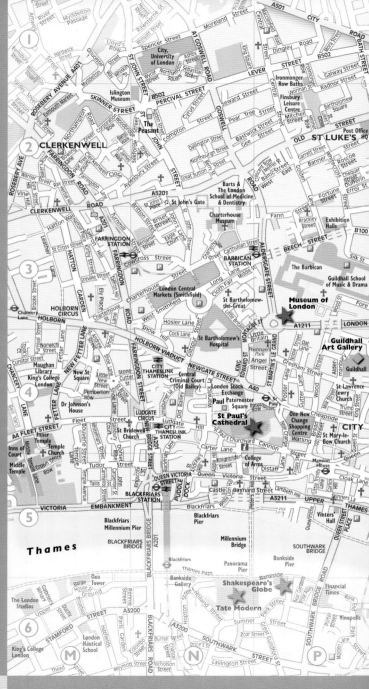

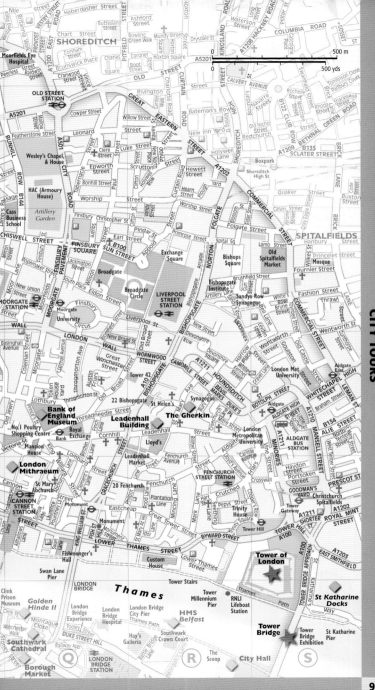

Fleet Street to the Tower
Quick Reference Guide

Museum of London (▷ 32)

There is no better place than this to get an overview of the city's history, from prehistoric times to the present day. Its fascinating exhibits include Roman and medieval treasures, plus the London 2012 Olympic Cauldron. The museum stands where the city first began, on the site of the Roman fort.

St. Paul's Cathedral (▷ 42)

Five monarchs oversaw the building of Sir Christopher Wren's masterpiece, completed in 1710, and ever since it has been the place where events of national importance are celebrated, mourned and commemorated. Come in the early evening to listen to the choir sing evensong.

Tower Bridge (▷ 56)

The most famous of London's bridges is a road bridge with a difference: the middle section between the two towers raises up to allow ships through. Visitors can explore inside the towers to see how it all works, then climb up to the high walkways between them for superb views.

Tower of London (▷ 58)

As it is one of London's most popular sights, it's definitely worth pre-booking your entry tickets for the Tower, especially during the high-season summer months. A tour with a Yeoman Warder (known as a Beefeater) as your guide is a unique experience.

CITY TOURS

St. Paul's and the Millennium Bridge

Covent Garden to Regent's Park

Literary associations, museums great and quirky, fine art and fun shopping all combine on this walk, which takes in busy streets and quiet corners. Here you'll find Theatreland, the heart of London's entertainment industry, lively Chinatown and Soho.

Morning

From Holborn Underground station, turn off Kingsway to enter Lincoln's Inn Fields. On its northern side, quirky **Sir John Soane's Museum** (left, ▷ 74) has a wonderful collection. As you cross the leafy square, look to the left to see the impressive brick buildings of Lincoln's Inn, one of the Inns of Court. With its outdoor terraces and open kitchen, **Fields Bar & Kitchen**, at the heart of Lincoln's Inn Fields, may tempt you to a coffee or breakfast, before continuing on to **The Old Curiosity Shop**, built in 1567, immortalized by Charles Dickens and now displaying handmade shoes. Following St. Clement's Lane will take you through the London School of Economics' campus and out alongside the Royal Courts of Justice to the Strand, where Wren's **St. Clement Danes Church** sits on an island amid busy traffic.

Mid-morning

Continue west along the Strand to **Somerset House** (▷ 48–49) to admire the great courtyard and its dancing fountains, and see what's on in the various exhibition galleries.

Lunch

Lunch in grand surroundings at Somerset House or walk up Wellington Street into lively **Covent Garden** (▷ 18–19), which is packed with cafés, restaurants and bars. **Joe Allen** (▷ 147–148) is a favorite. Turn left for the **Piazza**. Here you can shop and enjoy the buzz in the former market (right). Cross Long Acre for the trendy shops on Neal Street.

Afternoon

Passing the brightly colored high-rise blocks on St. Giles High Street, visit **St. Giles-in-the-Fields**, a handsome church with a Palladian interior, founded by Queen Matilda in 1101 as a leper hospital. Continue down Denmark Street, famed for its music connections and retaining some of its guitar shops, and cross Charing Cross Road with Foyles, London's famous bookshop, on the left, to reach leafy **Soho Square**. In the 17th century, this was one of the most fashionable places to live. Today the area is home to the film and recording industries and numerous pubs and restaurants.

Mid-afternoon

Leave at Frith Street, go right at **The Dog and Duck** pub (▷ 146), and stop for refreshment as you zigzag your way through cobbled Meard Street and across Wardour Street to the lively fruit and textiles **market** on Berwick Street. A left turn on Broadwick Street and another left down Lexington Street will take you to the specialist shops of Brewer Street and back onto Wardour Street. Cross Shaftesbury Avenue and turn left into Gerrard Street, the start of **Chinatown**.

Evening

Stroll through **Chinatown** (right) and pick a restaurant that takes your fancy. Shaftesbury Avenue is the heart of **Theatreland**, **Piccadilly Circus** is a short walk away and **Soho** buzzes with restaurants and nightlife.

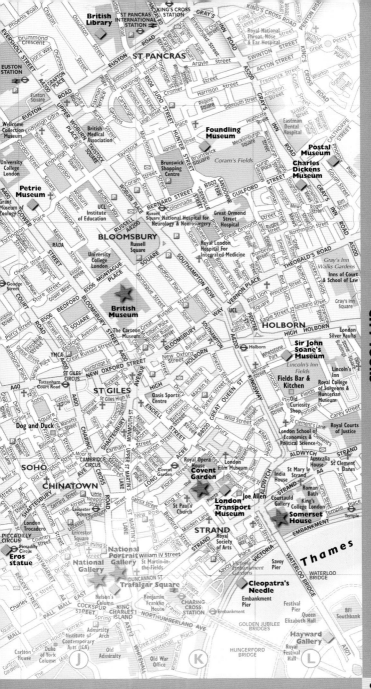

Covent Garden to Regent's Park
Quick Reference Guide

SIGHTS AND EXPERIENCES

British Museum (▷ 14)

This is one of the world's greatest museums, where you can travel the globe through exhibits from every civilization, spanning some two million years of human history. With eight million artifacts in the collection, special exhibitions, events, talks and activities, you may find you visit more than once.

Covent Garden (▷ 18)

With the Piazza at its heart and home to the Royal Opera House, this area is packed with stores, restaurants and lively street entertainment.

Somerset House (▷ 48)

In summer, fountains play in the courtyard; in winter it becomes a magical outdoor ice rink. Whenever you visit, there's likely to be something happening and there are plenty of options for eating and drinking.

MORE TO SEE   **64**

British Library
Charles Dickens Museum
Cleopatra's Needle
Eros statue
Foundling Museum
Handel & Hendrix in London
London Transport Museum
Madame Tussauds

Petrie Museum
Photographers' Gallery
Postal Museum
Regent's Park
Sir John Soane's Museum
Wallace Collection
ZSL London Zoo

CITY TOURS

CITY TOURS

Westminster and St. James's

Westminster Abbey, the Houses of Parliament, Buckingham Palace, Trafalgar Square—some of London's most famous landmarks are located in Westminster. Follow in the footsteps of royalty as you take in famous art galleries, London's prettiest royal park and some upscale shopping.

Morning
Begin your day at **Trafalgar Square** (▷ 75), where Sir Edwin Landseer's lions proudly protect Nelson's Column. Presiding over its northern side, the **National Gallery** (▷ 34–35) shows Western European art in a stately setting. Next door, the **National Portrait Gallery** (above, ▷ 36–37) puts faces to famous names down the centuries. Both galleries have good cafés, but you could also try the cozy **Café in the Crypt** at nearby **St. Martin-in-the-Fields** (▷ 138–139). Perhaps book for a candlelit concert while you are there.

Mid-morning
Walk down Whitehall to visit the **Banqueting House** (right, ▷ 66), noted for its Rubens ceiling, and to see **Horse Guards** and the **Cenotaph** war memorial. You soon arrive at **Big Ben** and the **Houses of Parliament** (▷ 22–23). There are splendid views of the River Thames from Westminster Bridge, immortalized by poet William Wordsworth and Impressionist Claude Monet. **Westminster Abbey** (▷ 62–63) lies across the square.

Lunch
Turn up Storey's Gate to **St. James's Park** (▷ 40–41), perhaps picking up a sandwich en route to eat in this pretty royal park. Alternatively, try **St. James's Café** (▷ 150–151). You will pass the **Churchill War Rooms** (▷ 67–68) beneath a sweeping flight of steps, watched over by the statue of an imperious Clive of India, and may wish to return there after lunch. Stroll among the park's trees and flowerbeds and watch the ducks, geese and pelicans feeding on the lake.

Afternoon

Crossing the Mall, a wide ceremonial route packed with crowds on great occasions, you will see **Buckingham Palace** (above, ▷ 16–17) on your left, fronted by the Queen Victoria Memorial. Walk up the Mall to get a closer look at the palace, or cross to Marlborough Road alongside the red-brick **St. James's Palace,** home of the Household Office of Prince William and Prince Harry. **Clarence House** (▷ 68), official London residence of Prince Charles and the Duchess of Cornwall, is on the far side of the palace.

Mid-afternoon

St. James's Street is lined with old-established businesses and famously exclusive members' clubs. Turn right into Jermyn Street for quintessentially British shops, many carrying the Royal Warrant. Walking through the elegant Piccadilly Arcade brings you into Piccadilly, where **Fortnum & Mason** (▷ 124) is the perfect place for afternoon tea. **Hatchards** (▷ 125), booksellers since 1797, is next door. Visit **St. James's, Piccadilly** (▷ 73), Wren's church for the local aristocracy. There may be a concert on there in the evening.

Evening

If you like the Grand Café tradition, **The Wolseley** (▷ 151) is for you. Or dress up for dinner at **Tamarind** (▷ 151) in Mayfair. As an alternative, reserve an evening **Thames River dinner cruise** (left, ▷ 54–55).

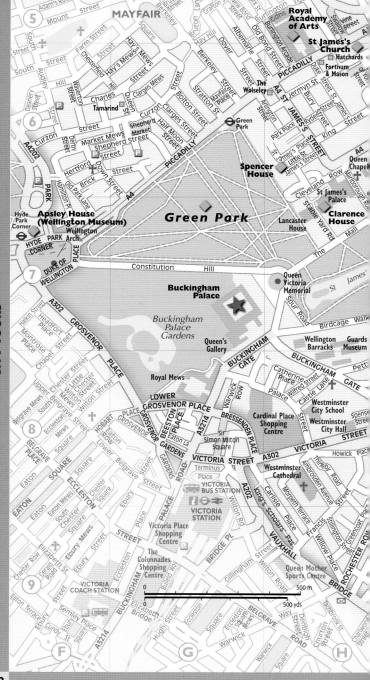

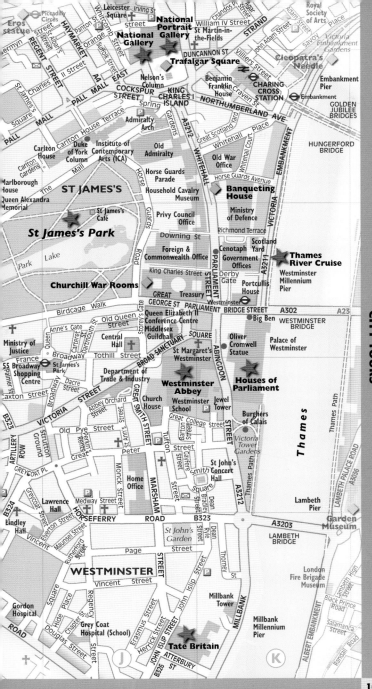

Westminster and St. James's
Quick Reference Guide

 SIGHTS AND EXPERIENCES

Buckingham Palace (▷ 16)
The summer opening of this royal residence and office of the Royal Household is not to be missed.

Houses of Parliament (▷ 22)
Britain is governed from this landmark Victorian Gothic building on the banks of the Thames.

National Gallery (▷ 34)
The superb collection gives an overview of European painting from Giotto to Cézanne.

National Portrait Gallery (▷ 36)
The famous and the infamous, past and present, are portrayed in paintings and photographs.

St. James's Park (▷ 40)
Tree-filled, surrounded by palaces and with a lake at its heart, this is the prettiest of the royal parks.

Tate Britain (▷ 50)
Tate Britain exhibits British art from 1500 to the 21st century, with a whole gallery devoted to Turner.

Thames River Cruise (▷ 54)
Sit down, relax and enjoy the views as you drift by some of London's best-known landmarks.

Westminster Abbey (▷ 62)
The vast abbey is full of exquisite detail and monuments—a grandiose pageant of British history.

MORE TO SEE 64

Apsley House
Banqueting House
Churchill War Rooms
Clarence House
Green Park

Royal Academy of Arts
St. James's, Piccadilly
Spencer House
Trafalgar Square

SHOP 118

Books
Hatchards
Department Stores
Fortnum & Mason

Fashion
Turnbull & Asser
Health and Beauty
Floris

ENTERTAINMENT 128

Comedy
The Comedy Store
Dancing
The Ritz
Film
Institute of Contemporary Arts
  (ICA)

Opera, Ballet and Concerts
St. James's, Piccadilly
St. Martin-in-the-Fields
Theaters
The Other Place
Victoria Palace Theatre

EAT 140

Asian
Tamarind
British and Modern
Portrait Restaurant
The Wolseley

Lighter Bites
St. James's Café

CITY TOURS

Around Hyde Park

A feast of world-class museums and music put South Kensington firmly on every visitor's must-see list. Adjoining Hyde Park, Kensington Gardens come complete with a romantic royal palace and memories of Diana, Princess of Wales, who lived there.

CITY TOURS

Morning

At **South Kensington Underground** station there's a passage marked "To the Museums." Follow it, or come up to street level for a fortifying breakfast at one of the many cafés and patisseries that crowd this popular area. You are heading for the Cromwell Road and three world-class museums: the **Victoria and Albert Museum** (left, ▷ 60–61), the **Natural History Museum** (▷ 38–39) and the **Science Museum** (▷ 44–45). They are free, so you could pop into each one to get an idea of their riches, or spend the morning engrossed in the subjects that interest you most.

Mid-morning

All three museums have **cafés** to retreat to for sustenance. One of the cafés at the V&A is located in what was the world's first museum restaurant, in rooms intended as a showpiece of modern design and craftsmanship. In summer you can eat outdoors. The cafés at the Science and Natural History museums are particularly child-friendly.

Lunch

Walk up Exhibition Road toward **Hyde Park** (▷ 71), turning left at Prince Consort Road to view the stately **Royal College of Music** and to approach the elliptical **Royal Albert Hall** (▷ 138). **Verdi–Italian Kitchen** upstairs is a good lunch spot, and you could perhaps make reservations for a concert or tour. Look at the detail on the frieze that rings this distinctive domed building and, going west, don't miss the reliefs and *sgraffito* that decorate the facade of the building opposite, previously occupied by the Royal College of Organists.

Afternoon

Cross Kensington Gore to the **Albert Memorial** (right, ▷ 66), an ornate fantasy in glittering gold by George Gilbert Scott. Stroll through **Kensington Gardens** (▷ 26–27) to the Diana, Princess of Wales Memorial Fountain in adjacent Hyde Park. Then take the path back through Kensington Gardens via the Round Pond to **Kensington Palace** (▷ 26–27).

Mid-afternoon

Tour Kensington Palace and take afternoon tea in the Kensington Palace Pavilion. Leaving by the Kensington Palace Gardens exit and "billionaires' row" of embassies, cross Kensington Church Street to the specialist shops and galleries along **Holland Street**. Turn left down **Kensington Church Walk** for exquisite little shops, courtyard houses and gardens. This is a secret, village-like London, yet it's only seconds away from busy Kensington High Street.

Dinner

Kensington favorite **Maggie Jones's** (▷ 148) is nearby, serving traditional dishes in a rustic, informal setting. If you fancy something smarter, you could take the bus to Knightsbridge, go shopping, then relax in the **Champagne Bar** at **Harrods** (below, ▷ 125).

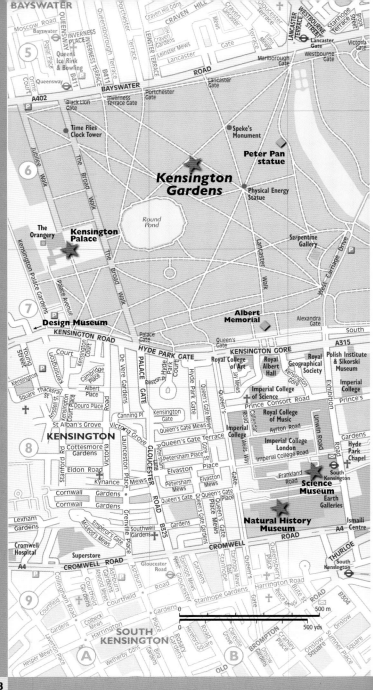

Moscow Road
Bayswater
Poplar Place
Queens
Ice Rink
& Bowling
Queensway
Orme Court
A402
Black Lion
Gate

QUEENSWAY
INVERNESS
PLACE
B411
INVERNESS TERRACE
Inverness
Terrace Gate
The Broad Walk

Porchester Terrace
Queensborough Terrace
Craven Hill Gdns
CRAVEN HILL
Craven
Lancaster
Leinster
Gardens
Leinster Mews
Leinster
Terrace
Lancaster

LEINSTER TERRACE

Gloucester

Craven
Terrace

LANCASTER TERRACE

WESTBOURNE STREET

STANHOPE STREET
BROOK STREET

ROAD

Lancaster
Gate

Marlborough
Gate

Westbourne
Gate

Lancaster
Gate

Lancaster
Gate
Victoria
Gate

BAYSWATER
Portchester
Gate

5

6

Jubilee Walk

Time Flies
Clock Tower

Speke's
Monument

Peter Pan
statue

*Kensington
Gardens*

Physical Energy
Statue

Round
Pond

Serpentine
Gallery

Lancaster Walk

West Carriage Drive

The Broad Walk

7

The
Orangery

**Kensington
Palace**

Kensington Palace Gardens

Palace Avenue

Design Museum

KENSINGTON ROAD

**Albert
Memorial**

Alexandra
Gate

Palace
Gate

HYDE PARK GATE

Queen's
Gate

KENSINGTON GORE

South

A315

8

Young Street

Kensington Court

Kensington Court
Cambridge
Place
Albert
Place
Douro Place

Thackeray St
Stanford Rd
St Alban's Grove

KENSINGTON

Cottesmore
Gardens
Eldon Road

Cornwall Gardens

Cornwall Gardens

De Vere Gardens

PALACE GATE

Victoria Grove

Canning Pl

Kensington
Gate

Queen's Gate Mews

Queen's Gate Terrace

Petersham Place
Elvaston
Place
Petersham
Mews
Elvaston
Mews

Launceston Place

GLOUCESTER ROAD

Kynance
Mews

Emperor's Gate

McLeod's Mews

Grenville Place

Southwell
Gardens

B325

Queen's Gate

Queen's Gate Place

Queen's Gate Place Mews

Queen's Gate Gardens

CROMWELL

Royal College
of Art

Royal
Albert
Hall

Royal
Geographical
Society

Polish Institute
& Sikorski
Museum

Imperial
College

Imperial College
of Science
Prince Consort Road

Royal College
of Music

Ayrton Road

Imperial
College

Imperial College
London

Imperial College Road

Prince's

Calendar Road

Jay Mews

Prince's

Kensington Gore

Wells Way

Unwin Road

Gardens

Hyde
Park
Chapel

Frankland
Road

**Science
Museum**

South
Kensington

Earth
Galleries

**Natural History
Museum**

ROAD

A4

Ismaili
Centre

9

Lexham
Gardens

Cromwell
Hospital
A4

Marloes Rd

Stratford Rd

Superstore

CROMWELL ROAD

Collingham Road

Courtfield
Gardens

Ashburn
Gardens

Ashburn
Mews

Ashburn Place

Gloucester
Road

Stanhope Gardens

Stanhope
Gardens

Queensberry
Place

THURLOE

South
Kensington

ROAD

B304

**SOUTH
KENSINGTON**

Courtfield
Gardens

Collingham Road

Hesper Mews

Harrington Gardens

Wetherby Gdns

Colbeck Mews

Gardens

Bina Gardens

Rosary
Gardens

Harrington Road

Reece Mews

Stanhope
Mews East

Cranley
Place

Clareville
Grove

OLD BROMPTON

Onslow
Square

Summer Place

Onslow Place

0   500 m

0   500 yds

A

B

CITY TOURS

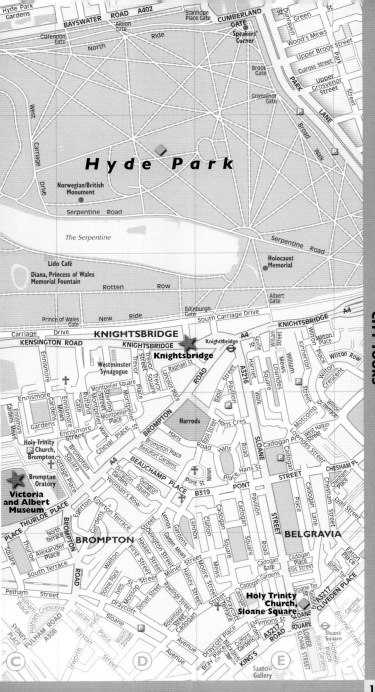

Hyde Park Gardens

BAYSWATER ROAD A402

Stanhope Place Gate

CUMBERLAND GATE

Albion Gate

Speakers' Corner

Clarendon Gate

Ride

Wood's Mews

Green St

Dunraven St

North

Upper Brook Street

West

Culross Street

Brook Gate

Upper Grosvenor Street

Carriage

Drive

Grosvenor Gate

PARK

LANE

Broad

Walk

Hyde Park

Norwegian/British Monument

Serpentine Road

The Serpentine

Serpentine Road

Lido Café

Holocaust Memorial

Diana, Princess of Wales Memorial Fountain

Rotten Row

Albert Gate

Prince of Wales Gate

New Ride

Edinburgh Gate

South Carriage Drive

KNIGHTSBRIDGE A4

Carriage Drive

KENSINGTON ROAD

KNIGHTSBRIDGE

KNIGHTSBRIDGE

Knightsbridge

A4

Sloane St

Seville

William

Wilton Place

Wilton Row

Wilton Crescent

Knightsbridge

Westminster Synagogue

Trevor Place

Trevor Street

Trevor Square

Raphael St

Lancelot Place

BROMPTON ROAD

A3216

Basil Street

Pavilion

Harriet Walk

Mews

Lowndes Square

William Street

Motcomb St

West Halkin Street

Lowndes Street

Wilton Terrace

Ennismore Gardens

Montpelier Square

Sterling St

Montpelier Walk

Montpelier St

Montpelier Place

Cheval Place

Hans

Road

Harrods

Hans Cres

Brompton Place

Hans Road

Hans Street

Hans Place

SLOANE STREET

Cadogan Lane

Cadogan Place

CHESHAM PL.

Chesham Place

Ennismore Mews

Ennismore Gardens Mews

Ennismore Street

Rutland Gate

Rutland Street

Cheval Place

Beauchamp Place

Brompton Place

Beaufort Gardens

Pont St Mews

PONT STREET

B319

Cadogan Gate

Cadogan Lane

Lyall Street

Chesham Street

Holy Trinity Church, Brompton

Brompton Square

A4

Cottage Place

Quinton Place

Ovington Gardens

Ovington Square

Yeoman's Row

Cadogan Square

Cadogan Gardens

Pavilion Road

BELGRAVIA

Eaton Place

Cadogan Place

Ellis Street

Brompton Oratory

Cottage Place

BEAUCHAMP PLACE

Lennox Gardens

Lennox Gardens Mews

Clabon Mews

Pont St

Victoria and Albert Museum

THURLOE PLACE

PLACE

BROMPTON ROAD

Egerton Gardens

Egerton Terrace

Ovington Street

First Street

Milner Street

Moore Street

Halsey Street

Cadogan Street

Cadogan Gardens

North Terrace

Alexander Place

South Terrace

Thurloe Square

Walton Street

Hasker Street

Denyer Street

Rawlings Street

Draycott Place

Draycott Avenue

BROMPTON

Egerton Terrace

Lennox Gardens

Ixworth Place

Pelham Street

Pelham Crescent

Pelham Place

Thurloe Square

Donne Place

Ives St.

Moscop Street

Draycott Avenue

Sloane Avenue

Lucan Place

Elystan Place

Makins Street

Rosemoor Street

Sydney Street

Cadogan

Bray Place

Culford Place

Coulson Street

Symons St

Draycott Place

Holy Trinity Church, Sloane Square

Sloane Ter

Sedding St

A3217

CLIVEDEN PLACE

SLOANE SQUARE

A3217 ROAD

KING'S

LOWER SLOANE STREET

Sloane Square

Sloane Gardens

Bourne Street

Caroline Terrace

Eaton Terrace

SYDNEY PLACE

FULHAM ROAD A308

Saatchi Gallery

© C

© D

© E

Around Hyde Park
Quick Reference Guide

TOP 25 SIGHTS AND EXPERIENCES

Kensington Palace and Gardens (▷ 26)
This historic royal residence, set in the beautiful 110ha (272-acre) Kensington Gardens, has been the home of Queen Victoria and Diana, Princess of Wales.

Knightsbridge Shopping (▷ 28)
Knightsbridge's shops enthrall the most dedicated fashionista, with window displays to delight the eye. Don't miss those famous London landmarks, Harvey Nichols and Harrods.

Natural History Museum (▷ 38)
With everything that you have ever wanted to know about the natural world and a whole lot more under one roof, the museum is a real family favorite.

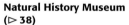

Science Museum (▷ 44)
With exhibits ranging from Stephenson's steam locomotive *Rocket* to a space capsule, and an IMAX cinema and plenty of hands-on fun, the museum makes science entertaining.

Victoria and Albert Museum (▷ 60)
This wonderful treasure house of decorative arts, one of the largest collections of its kind in the world, delights, inspires and often surprises.

MORE TO SEE

64

Albert Memorial
Design Museum
Holy Trinity, Sloane Square
Hyde Park
Peter Pan statue

SHOP

118

Department Stores
Harrods
Harvey Nichols
Peter Jones

Fashion
Brora
Jimmy Choo

ENTERTAINMENT

128

Film
Ciné Lumière
Opera, Ballet and Concerts
Cadogan Hall
Holland Park Theatre
Royal Albert Hall

Theaters
Royal Court/Jerwood Theatre
  Upstairs

EAT

140

Asian
Amaya
Royal China
British and Modern
Bibendum
Maggie Jones's

Famous Chefs
Le Gavroche

CITY TOURS

Farther Afield

Birthplace of Henry VIII and Elizabeth I, home to the National Maritime Museum and famed for the Royal Observatory, Greenwich (▷ 20–21) makes a great escape from central London, with open parkland, river views and a lively market selling food and crafts.

Morning

The perfect way to travel to Greenwich is by boat, as the royals did in centuries past, for the **Old Royal Naval College** (above, ▷ 20) presents a splendid baroque facade to the river. Alternatively, the Docklands Light Railway (DLR) gets you there quickly. Make your first stop the **Discover Greenwich** tourist information center, which has an excellent exhibition on the **Maritime Greenwich World Heritage Site** and the very good **Old Brewery** gastropub (tel 020 3437 2222). Located in the Pepys Building, it is close to the magnificent *Cutty Sark* (▷ 20), the world's last tea clipper, restored after serious fire damage.

Mid-morning

Cross Romney Road to visit the **National Maritime Museum** (right, ▷ 20–21) and delve into all matters nautical, with plenty of hands-on exhibits. A colonnade links the museum with the elegant Palladian-style **Queen's House**, designed by Inigo Jones in the 17th century. Today it houses a fine art collection with works by Gainsborough, Reynolds and Turner. Back across Romney Road, visit the neo-classical **Chapel of St. Peter and St. Paul** and the magnificent **Painted Hall** of the Old Royal Naval College. The ceiling here took 19 years to complete and the artist, James Thornhill, was eventually knighted for his labors. It was here that the body of Admiral Lord Nelson lay in state after the Battle of Trafalgar.

Lunch
Return to the **Old Brewery** in the Pepys Building. Alternatively, Greenwich Market in the center of town has plenty of inexpensive food stalls for a tasty lunch.

Afternoon
Now head up the hill in Greenwich Park to the **Royal Observatory** (above, ▷ 21), commissioned by Charles II and designed by Wren in 1675 with the purpose of finding longitude at sea. The Time galleries' exhibits, interactive **Astronomy Centre** and the **Peter Harrison Planetarium** are fascinating. Here you can stand astride the **Greenwich Meridian** line.

Mid-afternoon
Covering 74ha (183 acres) **Greenwich Park** is the oldest enclosed royal park, with rose gardens, a flower garden, lake, wilderness deer park and fine views across the Thames to Docklands and the City of London (left). Follow a path leading to Regency houses on Crooms Hill and continue downhill to the lively weekend **market**, packed with food stalls, crafts and small design shops.

Dinner
Take the DLR to **Canary Wharf** (▷ 76), in the heart of Docklands, to eat at the 18th-century waterside pub **The Gun** (▷ 147), once the haunt of smugglers and Lord Nelson's favorite trysting place.

Stanmore

A410

Edgware

A41

A409

A4140

A5

M1

A1

A1000

Finchley

A406

Alexandra
Park

Hendon

A1

Fryent
Country
Park

Kenwood

**Highgate
Cemetery**

Golders
Hill Park

**Hampstead
Heath**

A404

A4005

Wembley

A406

A41

A5

Willesden

**Primrose
Hill**

**Jewish
Museum**

A40

A406

Kilburn

Regent's
Park

A404

Paddington

A40

Wormwood
Scrubs Park

**Portobello
Road Market**

Kensington
Gardens

Hyde Park

Green
Park

EALING

A4020

Holland
Park

A4020

HAMMERSMITH

WESTMINSTER

A3002

M4

A4

**Chiswick
House**

**Chelsea
Physic
Garden**

Syon
Park

**Kew
Gardens**

Battersea
Park

Thames

Clapham

RICHMOND

Putney

WANDSWORTH

Clapham
Common

A3

Richmond
Park

A316

Wandsworth
Common

A214

A3

Tooting
Bec
Common

A24

**Ham House
and Garden**

Ham
Common

A307

A308

Wimbledon
Common

A3

Streatham

A216

A310

**KINGSTON
UPON THAMES**

Wimbledon

A238

MERTON

Bushy
Park

Morden
Hall
Park

Mitcham

Hampton
Court Park

A2043

Morden

Mitcham
Common

A309

A24

Beddington
Park

A3

A217

A240

A243

A232

A237

SUTTON

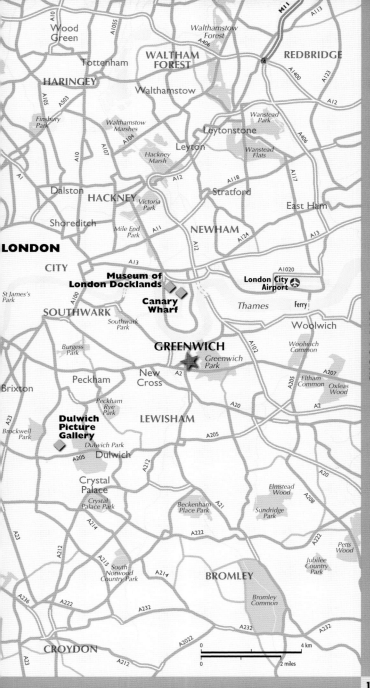

SIGHTS AND EXPERIENCES

Greenwich (▷ 20)

The ideal way to spend a Sunday is to take a cruise on the Thames to Greenwich, a UNESCO World Heritage Site. Visit the great maritime sights and the Royal Observatory, take a leisurely stroll in historic Greenwich Park and shop in the lively crafts market.

MORE TO SEE	64

Canary Wharf
Chelsea Physic Garden
Chiswick House
Dulwich Picture Gallery
Ham House and Garden
Hampstead Heath
Highgate Cemetery

Jewish Museum
Kenwood
Kew Gardens
Museum of London Docklands
Portobello Road Market
V&A Museum of Childhood

SHOP	118

Books
Books for Cooks
Homeware
Contemporary Applied Arts

Shopping Centers
Westfield London
Street Markets
Camden Markets

Shop

Whether you're looking for the best local products, a department store or a quirky boutique, you'll find them all in London. In this section shops are listed alphabetically.

SHOP

Introduction

A city influenced by global cultures, with a history of producing excellent design, style and fashion, London offers some of the world's greatest and most varied choices for shopping. Here, you'll find saris and spices as easily as rare reggae records, depending on the district—it really pays to explore beyond the West End. For shoppers, the choice ranges from vibrant street markets to legendary department stores and from offbeat boutiques to smart galleries of paintings and antiques.

Contemporary and Traditional
It is the extraordinary range that excites visitors. London has outrageous fashion, bolstered by the annual crop of imaginative art-, fashion- and design-school graduates. By contrast, long-established shopping streets, such as Oxford Street and Kensington High Street, offer major brands, while markets such as Camden Lock and Portobello Road are eclectic, ethnic, independent and inexpensive.

Buying a London Memory
London's souvenirs range from tatty to tasteful. Ever since the Swinging Sixties, anything with a Union Jack flag on it has sold well. For high

BEST OF BRITISH

Take home some British souvenirs with a difference. You can buy beautifully crafted umbrellas and walking sticks from James Smith & Sons (✉ 53 New Oxford Street, WC1). For a good British cheese buy a Stilton, all ready and packed, from Paxton & Whitfield (✉ 93 Jermyn Street, SW1). If you want to try some British recipes go to Books for Cooks (✉ 4 Blenheim Crescent, W11) for a large selection of cookbooks. Tea addicts should head to The Tea House (✉ 15 Neal Street, WC2) for a choice of blends and some stylish teapots. For bespoke stationery and leather goods, Smythson of Bond Street (✉ 131 New Bond Street, W1) is the epitome of elegance.

Clockwise from top: The elegant arcades of Leadenhall Market; handmade shoes for sale in St. James's; one of the antiques shops in Camden Passage; the central well

quality, go to the museum shops. Gifts at the shop in Buckingham Palace Mews include the Queen Victoria range of china, a mini-crown for a charm bracelet or a guardsman mug. The Victoria and Albert Museum, British Museum and National Gallery also stock quality items inspired by their diverse collections—budget permitting, you can do a full-scale family gift shop at any of these. Tate Modern has fine handcrafted jewelry, while the Museum of London is particularly good for souvenirs and books about London. At the National Portrait Gallery, you will find books on historical figures and British history, as well as a good supply of postcards and posters.

The Ultimate British Buy

Go to St. James's or Knightsbridge to purchase traditional British-made goods such as tweed jackets, handmade shoes or elegant china, delicate fragrances, floral-printed fabrics and cashmere sweaters. Visit Burlington Arcade (▷ panel below) for its specialist upscale shops in a historic setting. Burberry and Aquascutum are synonymous with raincoats. Harrods has been trading for some 150 years; Selfridges was the country's first department store and is the second largest after Harrods; and Liberty fabrics are still exotic and luxurious. The winter and summer sales are major events in any serious shopper's diary.

SHOP

SHOP THE SHOP

Charles Dickens would recognize many London shops today. Burlington Arcade, off Piccadilly, is an 18th-century covered shopping mall, with a liveried beadle to maintain decorum. Many shops display the royal insignia, showing that they supply members of the Royal Household with everything from brushes to jewels (royalwarrant.org). For instance, John Lobb (✉ 9 St. James's Street, SW1) custom-makes shoes and boots for the royal family—and for you, at a price.

in Liberty; Lobb on St. James's Street, selling exclusive made-to-measure shoes; Fortnum & Mason in Piccadilly, renowned for its luxury foods and top-notch wines

Directory

SHOP

FLEET STREET TO THE TOWER
Fashion
The Goodhood Store
Luna & Curious
Food and Drink
Paul
Shopping Centers
Royal Exchange
Markets
Leadenhall Market

COVENT GARDEN TO REGENT'S PARK
Art and Antiques
Grays Antiques Market
Books
Daunt Books
Stanfords
Department Stores
Liberty
Selfridges
Fashion
The Cambridge Satchel Company
Health and Beauty
Neal's Yard Remedies
Homeware
Aram Designs Ltd
Designers Guild
Heal's
Thomas Goode Ltd
Toys
Benjamin Pollock's Toyshop
Hamleys

WESTMINSTER AND ST. JAMES'S
Books
Hatchards
Department Stores
Fortnum & Mason
Fashion
Turnbull & Asser
Health and Beauty
Floris

AROUND HYDE PARK
Department Stores
Harrods
Harvey Nichols
Peter Jones
Fashion
Brora
Jimmy Choo

FARTHER AFIELD
Books
Books for Cooks
Homeware
Contemporary Applied Arts
Shopping Centers
Westfield London
Street Markets
Camden Markets

Shopping A–Z

ARAM DESIGNS LTD

aram.co.uk

Displayed over five floors, the latest, most innovative designs in top-quality furniture and lighting can be seen here, created by internationally renowned designers and talented new graduates from all areas of the applied arts.

➕ L4 ✉ 110 Drury Lane, WC2 ☎ 020 7557 7557 🕐 Mon–Sat 10–6 (Thu until 7) 🚇 Covent Garden

BENJAMIN POLLOCK'S TOYSHOP

pollocks-coventgarden.co.uk

Selling traditional toy theaters, paper models, puppets, music boxes and all kinds of collectible toys, this Covent Garden stalwart is delightfully old school.

➕ K5 ✉ 44 The Market, WC2 ☎ 020 7379 7866 🕐 Mon–Wed 10.30–6, Thu–Sat 10.30–6.30, Sun 11–6 🚇 Covent Garden

BOOKS FOR COOKS

booksforcooks.com

Browse the amazing selection of books about cooking and cuisine, then head to the café, where recipes are tested. Classes are held in the demonstration kitchen.

➕ Off map ✉ 4 Blenheim Crescent, W11 ☎ 020 7221 1992 🕐 Tue–Sat 10–6. Closed last 3 weeks in Aug and 10 days over Christmas 🚇 Ladbroke Grove

BRORA

brora.co.uk

Choose from cashmere in an array of rich and subtle shades for men, women and children. Plain or patterned, it is expensive, but the quality is superb.

➕ E9 ✉ 6–8 Symons Street, SW3 ☎ 020 7730 2665 🕐 Mon–Sat 10–6, Sun 11–5 🚇 Sloane Square

THE CAMBRIDGE SATCHEL COMPANY

cambridgesatchel.com

Handmade and quintessentially British, the top-quality leather bags sold here are design classics. From cross-body bags to backpack styles and totes, they come in a variety of sizes and colors and can even be personalized with your initials.

➕ K5 ✉ 31 James Street, WC2 ☎ 020 3077 1100 🕐 Mon–Fri 10–8, Sat 10–7, Sun 11–6 🚇 Covent Garden

CAMDEN MARKET

camdenmarket.com

Source of all things funky and fun, with an eclectic mix of stores and stalls, this is the place to head for vintage clothing and design, futuristic clubwear, tribal jewelry, reggae records, handmade accessories and alternative gifts, plus street food, bars and cult cafés. It's at its height on the weekend.

➕ Off map ✉ Camden Lock Place, NW1 🕐 Daily 10–approx 7; times vary for each business 🚇 Camden Town, Chalk Farm

CONTEMPORARY APPLIED ARTS

caa.org.uk

Dedicated to promoting British artists, the CAA shop displays outstanding contemporary crafts, from

PRIVATE GALLERIES

An indispensable tool to help you find out more about commercial art galleries in London is the excellent monthly *Galleries* magazine (galleries.co.uk), which is available free from most galleries. With its maps and specialist subject index, information can be called up by area as well as subject.

ceramics, glass and textiles to jewelry, metalwork and wood.
➕ N6 ✉ 89 Southwark Street, SE1 ☎ 020 7620 0086 ⏱ Mon–Sat 10–6 🚇 Southwark, Blackfriars

DAUNT BOOKS
dauntbooks.co.uk
The glorious Marylebone flagship of the independent bookseller has Edwardian oak balconies and a long main room with stained-glass windows. The specialty is travel, with titles organized by country.
➕ F3 ✉ 83 Marylebone High Street, W1 ☎ 020 7224 2295 ⏱ Mon–Sat 9–7.30, Sun 11–6 🚇 Baker Street, Bond Street

DESIGNERS GUILD
designersguild.com
Tricia Guild's store is a wonderland of exquisite design, with a range of modern china, glass and fabrics.
➕ F3 ✉ 76 Marylebone High Street, W1 ☎ 020 3301 5826 ⏱ Mon–Sat 10–6 (Thu until 7), Sun 11–5 🚇 Baker Street

FLORIS
florislondon.com
Creating fragrances since 1730, this original shop has oak-paneled counters and a sense of history and tradition. Scented candles are a luxurious treat for the home.

➕ H6 ✉ 89 Jermyn Street, SW1 ☎ 020 7747 3612 ⏱ Mon–Sat 9.30–6.30, Sun 11.30–5.30 🚇 Green Park, Piccadilly Circus

FORTNUM & MASON
fortnumandmason.com
Before venturing into London's premier grocer's shop, do not miss the clock, which has Messrs. Fortnum and Mason edging forward each hour. The shop-brand goods make perfectly delicious presents.
➕ H6 ✉ 181 Piccadilly, W1 ☎ 020 7734 8040 ⏱ Mon–Sat 10–9, Sun 12–6 🚇 Piccadilly Circus, Green Park

THE GOODHOOD STORE
goodhoodstore.com
This award-winning retailer sells more than 200 brands, spanning menswear, womenswear, lifestyle and beauty. The emphasis is on contemporary style and luxury.
➕ R1 ✉ 151 Curtain Road, EC2 ☎ 020 7729 3600 ⏱ Mon–Fri 10.30–6.30, Sat 10.30–7, Sun 12–6 🚇 Old Street

GRAYS ANTIQUES MARKET
graysantiques.com
In a labyrinthine building, the headquarters of 19th-century toilet manufacturers John Bolding and Son, more than 200 dealers sell antiques, clothing, objets d'art, fine jewelry, and vintage collectibles.
➕ F5 ✉ 58 Davies Street, W1 ☎ 020 7629 7034 ⏱ Mon–Fri 10–6, Sat 11–5 🚇 Bond Street

HAMLEYS
hamleys.com
In business for more than 250 years and probably the world's most famous toy shop, Hamleys has five action-packed floors, each dedicated to a different category.

⊞ H5 ✉ 188–196 Regent Street, W1
☎ 0371 704 1977 🕐 Mon–Fri 10–9,
Sat 9.30–9, Sun 12–6 Ⓜ Oxford Circus,
Piccadilly Circus

HARRODS
harrods.com
This vast emporium contains everything from designer fashions to luxury gifts and accessories, plus several restaurants, bars and spas.
⊞ D8 ✉ 87–135 Brompton Road, SW1
☎ 020 7730 1234 🕐 Mon–Sat 10–9,
Sun 11.30–6 Ⓜ Knightsbridge

HARVEY NICHOLS
harveynichols.com
Designer fashion, decadent jewelry, indulgent beauty, luxury food and drink—elegance and style are assured in the store that bags the title London's classiest clothes shop. It also has a popular restaurant.
⊞ E7 ✉ 109–125 Knightsbridge, SW1
☎ 020 7235 5000 🕐 Mon–Sat 10–8,
Sun 11.30–6 Ⓜ Knightsbridge

HATCHARDS
hatchards.co.uk
Booksellers since 1797, Hatchards is the oldest bookshop in London and is still in its original building.
⊞ H6 ✉ 187 Piccadilly, W1 ☎ 020 7439 9921 🕐 Mon–Sat 9.30–8, Sun 12–6.30 Ⓜ Piccadilly Circus, Green Park

---

AUCTION HOUSES

A visit to one of London's auction houses, even just to view, is an experience. Try Bonhams (✉ 101 New Bond Street, W1 ☎ 020 7447 7447, bonhams.com), Christie's (✉ 8 King Street, SW1 ☎ 020 7839 9060, christies.com) or Sotheby's (✉ 34 New Bond Street, W1 ☎ 020 7293 5000, sothebys.com).

HEAL'S
heals.com
A front-runner of the 1920s Arts and Crafts movement, Heal's specializes in timeless, modern designer furniture and homewares.
⊞ H3 ✉ 196 Tottenham Court Road, W1
☎ 020 7636 1666 🕐 Mon–Sat 10–7,
Thu 10–8, Sun 12–6 Ⓜ Goodge Street

JIMMY CHOO
jimmychoo.com
A fashionista heaven, Jimmy Choo in Knightsbridge is the place to buy the highest-heeled shoes in the latest styles in town.
⊞ E8 ✉ 32 Sloane Street, SW3 ☎ 020 7823 1051 🕐 Mon–Sat 10–7, Sun 12–5 Ⓜ Knightsbridge

Vibrant Leadenhall Market

MAKE A PICNIC

With so many parks and benches, London is a great place to picnic. The big stores have seductive food halls and stock wine; see Harrods, Selfridges and Fortnum & Mason. Berwick Street Market has myriad tempting food stalls, as of course does that foodie heaven, Borough Market (► 66–67).

LEADENHALL MARKET

leadenhallmarket.co.uk

This surprising City treat is housed under Sir Horace Jones's magnificent 19th-century wrought-iron and glass arcades. Quality food shops, boutiques, pubs and restaurants sit behind the traditional shop fronts on cobbled streets.

➕ R4 ✉ Gracechurch Street, EC3 🕐 Mon–Fri 10–6. Individual shops may differ 🚇 Bank, Monument

LIBERTY

libertylondon.com

With everything from sumptuous fabrics to china and glass, this shop is characterized by exoticism and cutting-edge fashion, with an Arts and Crafts heritage.

➕ G4 ✉ Regent Street, W1 ☎ 020 7734 1234 🕐 Mon–Sat 10–8, Sun 11.30–6 🚇 Oxford Circus

LUNA & CURIOUS

lunaandcurious.com

Some of London's most innovative shops are in Shoreditch (► 6–7) and this creative independent hub is worth seeking out for fashion, jewelry, accessories and homewares.

➕ S2 ✉ 24–26 Calvert Avenue, E2 ☎ 020 3222 0034 🕐 Mon–Sat 11–6, Sun 11–5 🚇 Old Street

NEAL'S YARD REMEDIES

nealsyardremedies.com

Believing in "beauty with no nasties," Neal's Yard specializes in organic, plant-based cosmetics and skincare products, and aromatherapy oils.

➕ K4 ✉ 15 Neal's Yard, WC2 ☎ 020 7379 7222 🕐 Mon–Sat 10–8, Sun 11–6.30 🚇 Covent Garden

PAUL

paul-uk.com

This iconic French bakery offers a tempting array of tarts, cakes, artisanal breads and chocolates, as well as filled baguettes and salads for a tasty lunch on the go.

➕ N4 ✉ 2 Paternoster Square, EC4 ☎ 020 7329 4705 🕐 Mon–Fri 7–7, Sat–Sun 8–7 🚇 St. Paul's

PETER JONES

johnlewis.com

This department store sells everything from fashion to homewares, and offers great views from the café and cocktail bar.

➕ E9 ✉ Sloane Square, SW1 ☎ 020 7730 3434 🕐 Mon–Sat 9.30–7 (Wed until 8), Sun 12–6 🚇 Sloane Square

ROYAL EXCHANGE

theroyalexchange.co.uk

William Tite's City landmark is now a beautiful shopping mall, where boutiques stock luxury gifts, watches, jewelry, fine art, handcrafted leather goods, stationery and designer fashion, and the dining options are equally stylish.

➕ Q4 ✉ Cornhill ☎ 020 7283 8935 🕐 For individual stores see website; restaurants and bars 8am–11pm 🚇 Bank

SELFRIDGES

selfridges.com

You could spend a whole day in this flagship store where every department is appealing, from the fashion floors to the superb food hall. There's also a range of restaurants and cafés for when you need to a refreshment break.

🚇 F4 ✉ 400 Oxford Street, W1 ☎ 0800 123 400 🕐 Mon–Sat 9.30–9, Sun 11.30–6 Ⓜ Marble Arch, Bond Street

STANFORDS

stanfords.co.uk

In business since 1853 and in the same location on Long Acre since 1901, the world's largest map retailer has a vast selection of travel guides and books, along with globes, children's books, gifts, stationery and travel accessories, plus a good little café.

🚇 K5 ✉ 12–14 Long Acre, WC2 ☎ 020 7836 1321 🕐 Mon–Sat 9–8, Sun 11.30–6 Ⓜ Covent Garden, Leicester Square

THOMAS GOODE LTD

thomasgoode.com

Collectors of bone china, fine glassware and cutlery need look no farther than this splendid showroom. Styles range from contemporary and classic to ultimate luxury.

🚇 F6 ✉ 19 South Audley Street, W1 ☎ 020 7499 2823 🕐 Mon–Sat 10–6 Ⓜ Green Park, Bond Street

TURNBULL & ASSER

turnbullandasser.co.uk

If you love classic British design, then the made-to-measure or off-the-peg men's shirts here are for you. The range is complemented by ties and accessories. Quality and service are superb.

SHOPPING SECRETS

For streets full of character, try Blenheim Crescent in Notting Hill, W11; Kensington Church Street, W8, renowned for its antiques shops and galleries; and Marylebone High Street, W1, with food, fashion and Oxfam's flagship books and music shop. Secreted off Oxford Street, Gees Court and St. Christopher's Place are fashion favorites.

🚇 H6 ✉ 71–72 Jermyn Street, SW1 ☎ 020 7808 3000 🕐 Mon–Fri 9–6, Sat 9.30–6 Ⓜ Green Park, Piccadilly Circus

WESTFIELD LONDON

uk.westfield.com/london

Westfield has more than 300 shops spanning designer and high-street labels, department stores and boutiques, plus restaurants and a multiplex cinema. Westfield Stratford City, even larger, is located by the Olympic site.

🚇 Off map ✉ Ariel Way, W12 ☎ 020 7061 1400 🕐 Mon–Sat 10–10, Sun 12–6 (some stores may vary) Ⓜ Shepherd's Bush, Wood Lane

The mock Tudor galleries at Liberty

SHOP

Entertainment

Once you've done with sightseeing for the day, you'll find lots of other great things to do with your time in this chapter, even if all you want to do is relax with a drink. In this section establishments are listed alphabetically.

Introduction

When darkness falls, London's pace doesn't let up, and there's a huge choice of lively nightclubs, bars and pubs where you can mingle with the locals.

Entertainment

London's Theatreland, with its big-budget West End musicals and plays starring renowned actors, is famed worldwide, but there's a great deal happening in smaller venues all over town, including alternative theater, comedy and cabaret. Hundreds of concerts take place every week in a variety of buildings, but especially churches, such as St. Martin-in-the-Fields, where the quality of lunchtime and evening recitals is very high and admission is nominal or free. A recently developed cultural landmark is Kings Place (tel 020 7520 1490, kingsplace.co.uk) in the revitalized area of King's Cross. There are opera, ballet and modern dance seasons in memorable locations, too, plus an array of fun festivals, especially during the summer months and the long public holiday weekends.

Film

As well as the big-screen cinemas in the West End showing the latest blockbuster movies, London has some very good venues screening art-house and indie films. The BFI Southbank

WALK THE WALK

The 2km-long (1-mile) stretch of riverside on the South Bank between Westminster Bridge and London Bridge bustles by night, as well as by day. The London Eye is magical after dusk. On the opposite bank, illuminated landmarks include the Houses of Parliament and Somerset House. At Oxo Tower Wharf, go to the top floor for a drink or a meal—there are few better views of London. Admire the Tate Modern (open until 10pm Friday and Saturday) and the Globe, then rest your feet at a riverside pub and enjoy spectacular views.

Clockwise from top: The Garrick Theatre in the West End; the Theatre Royal on Haymarket; the BFI IMAX on the South Bank; Shakespeare's Globe, a re-creation of

(▷ 133), which hosts the annual London Film Festival in October, Ciné Lumière (▷ 134), the Electric Cinema in Notting Hill (electriccinema.co.uk), the Curzon Mayfair and Curzon Bloomsbury (curzoncinemas.com) are all well worth visiting.

Summer Living

In the summer, London's outdoors comes into its own. Londoners enjoy concerts in beautiful settings such as Hampton Court Palace, Kenwood, Hyde Park and Kew Gardens, often bringing picnics with them. The music ranges from classical and opera to jazz and rock. Bars, pubs and cafés spill onto the city's streets, and many serve good food.

Clubs, Pubs and Bars

Year-round, the diversity of the club scene is legendary, with many changing themes; check what's on before you go. There are tried-and-tested venues and a host of pulsing new wave options. London's extensive bar scene ranges from cocktails at the elegant Savoy (▷ 159) or the upscale Blue Bar at The Berkeley (▷ 156) to Irish bars, sports bars and traditional street-corner pubs. You'll find some are in warrens of Tudor rooms; others take pride in their authentic Victorian and Edwardian decorations.

ENTERTAINMENT

LANDMARK CLUBBING

A mix of global names, trailblazing bands and DJs make Xoyo (✉ 32–37 Cowper Street, EC2 ☎ 020 7608 2878, xoyo.co.uk) a popular Shoreditch venue. Nearby is Village Underground (✉ 54 Holywell Lane, EC2A, villageunderground.co.uk), with its distinctive Tube carriages on the roof. Fabric (▷ 135) is a longstanding clubbers' favorite, attracting top DJs. Under Blackfriars Bridge, Pulse (✉ Invicta Plaza, SE1 ☎ 020 7261 0981, pulse-club.co.uk) is a huge state-of-the-art club space, with hi-tech sound and video mapping.

an Elizabethan playhouse; Young Dancer, *a bronze by Enzo Plazzotta outside the Royal Opera House in Covent Garden*

Directory

Entertainment A–Z

606 CLUB

606club.co.uk

West London's best small jazz club books British-based musicians with impeccable credentials. Alcohol is served only with food and the music cover charge is added to the cost of the meal.

⊞ Off map ⊠ 90 Lots Road, SW10 ☎ 020 7352 5953 🕐 Nightly daily plus Sun lunch 🚇 Earl's Court then bus C3, Fulham Broadway

BARBICAN CENTRE

barbican.org.uk

At Europe's largest multi-arts venue, world-famous orchestras and singers appear in the concert hall, while its two theaters stage innovative plays and dance productions. The center also has cinemas and art galleries, and hosts talks and events, with plentiful venues to eat and drink.

⊞ P3 ⊠ Silk Street, EC2 ☎ 020 7638 8891 🚇 Barbican

BFI IMAX

bfi.org.uk/bfi-imax

Watch exhilarating 2D and 3D movies on the biggest screen in Britain in this 500-seat cinema in a space-age setting.

⊞ L6 ⊠ 1 Charlie Chaplin Walk, South Bank, SE1 ☎ 0330 333 7878 🚇 Waterloo

BFI SOUTHBANK

bfi.org.uk

See both classic and new movies at this four-screen cinema which is famed for its seasons, events and director and actor retrospectives. It has a great shop and Mediatheque. Discounted tickets are often available.

⊞ L6 ⊠ South Bank, SE1 ☎ 020 7928 3232 🕐 Daily 9.45am–11pm 🚇 Waterloo

BORDERLINE

borderline.london

The hottest indie and rock bands strut their stuff at the venerable Borderline, recently refurbished.

⊞ J4 ⊠ Orange Yard, off Manette Street, W1 ☎ 020 3871 7777 🕐 Mon–Sat until late for gigs or club nights 🚇 Tottenham Court Road

THE BRIDGE THEATRE

bridgetheatre.co.uk

This 900-seater theater opened in late 2017 and focuses on the commission and production of exciting new shows, plus the occasional classic.

⊞ R6 ⊠ 3 Potters Field Park, SE1 ☎ 0333 320 0052 🕐 Performance times vary, check website 🚇 London Bridge

THE BULL'S HEAD

thebullsheadbarnes.com

This cozy riverside pub in Barnes serves good food and live music nightly and some Sunday lunchtimes—mainly jazz in its dedicated Jazz Room; check the website to see who is playing.

⊞ Off map ⊠ 373 Lonsdale Road, SW13 ☎ 020 8876 5241 🕐 Mon–Fri 11am–11pm, Sat 12–11, Sun 12–10; jazz nightly from 7–11pm 🚇 Barnes Bridge

THEATER TIPS

If you care about where you sit, you can usually find a seating plan online. For an evening "sold out" performance, it is worth waiting in line for returns; otherwise, try for a matinée. The cheapest seats may be far from the stage, uncomfortable or have a restricted view, so take binoculars and a cushion. Londoners rarely dress up for the theater but they might order their intermission drinks before the play starts.

The famed Comedy Store

BUSH HALL
bushhallmusic.co.uk
Listen to jazz, rock, folk or classics performed by famous names and upcoming artists at this ornate Edwardian dance hall, with a rock 'n' roll history as a rehearsal space for the likes of The Who and Adam Faith in the 1960s.
➕ Off map ✉ 310 Uxbridge Road, Shepherd's Bush, W12 ☎ 020 8222 6955
🕐 Shows: 7.30pm; see website for listings
Ⓢ Shepherd's Bush Market

CADOGAN HALL
cadoganhall.com
The Royal Philharmonic is the resident orchestra at this excellent venue that attracts international touring orchestras as well as staging contemporary folk, jazz and

world music concerts, talks and events. The hall is home to the BBC Proms Chamber Music series.
➕ E9 ✉ 5 Sloane Terrace, SW1 ☎ 020 7730 4500 Ⓢ Sloane Square

CINÉ LUMIÈRE
institut-francais.org.uk/cine-lumiere/
Part of the French government's hub of language and culture, Ciné Lumière shows French films as well as other European and world cinema.
➕ B9 ✉ Institut Français, 17 Queensberry Place, SW7 ☎ 020 7871 3515 🕐 Daily 10–9.30. Closed Aug Ⓢ South Kensington

THE COMEDY STORE
thecomedystore.co.uk
The best in stand-up comedy features improvised sketches from the Comedy Store Players, sharp, topical comedy from the Cutting Edge team and visiting talent from around the globe. Many big names in British TV and radio have started out here.
➕ J5 ✉ 1a Oxendon Street, SW1 ☎ 020 7024 2060 🕐 Shows nightly but times vary. Booking advisable Ⓢ Piccadilly Circus, Leicester Square

DONMAR WAREHOUSE
donmarwarehouse.com
Awards continue to flood in for this theater with just 250 bench-style seats and a record of innovative

productions, from Shakespeare to exciting new writing. Check for inexpensive standing tickets.

🚇 K4 ✉ 41 Earlham Street, WC2 🕐 Show times vary Ⓜ Covent Garden

FABRIC

fabriclondon.com

This hugely popular superclub, going strong since 1999, has three rooms—two with stages for live acts—dedicated to cutting-edge house, techno, electronica and bass-driven dance music. One of these has a "bodysonic" dance-floor that allows dancers to literally feel the music through their feet.

🚇 N3 ✉ 77a Charterhouse Street, EC1 ☎ 020 7336 8898 🕐 Fri–Sun from 11pm Ⓜ Farringdon

HOLLAND PARK THEATRE

operahollandpark.com

This is the venue for highly acclaimed opera, not theater, staged in summer (June–July) beneath a temporary canopy sheltering an auditorium of 1,000 seats in one of London's most romantic parks.

🚇 Off map ✉ Holland Park, W8 ☎ 0300 999 1000 Ⓜ Holland Park, High Street Kensington

INSTITUTE OF CONTEMPORARY ARTS (ICA)

ica.art

This cultural hotspot exhibits cutting-edge art, screens arty films and plays host to performance artists charting new territory in all media. There's a great bar-restaurant on site as well as a shop.

🚇 J6 ✉ The Mall, SW1 ☎ 020 7930 3647 🕐 Tue–Sun, exhibitions 12–9, bar-restaurant 12–late Ⓜ Piccadilly Circus, Charing Cross

THE JAZZ CAFÉ

thejazzcafelondon.com

Buzzing nightly with jazz, soul, R&B or funk, this venue in Camden has live acts or club nights daily, and a mezzanine restaurant that offers great views of the live show.

🚇 Off map ✉ 5 Parkway, NW1 ☎ 020 7485 6834 🕐 Daily 7pm–late Ⓜ Camden Town

KIA OVAL

kiaoval.com

Home to Surrey County Cricket Club, The Oval was the first ground in England to host international Test cricket, and in 2017 it hosted its 100th Test match. Watch county matches and world stars in action (May–September) here or join a tour of the ground year-round.

🚇 Off map ✉ Surrey County Cricket Club, Kennington, SE11 ☎ 020 3946 0100 Ⓜ Oval

KOKO

koko.uk.com

Since 1890, this venue has been through many incarnations. Today, go for hip-hop, pop and rock bands and partying under the gigantic mirror ball.

🚇 Off map ✉ 1a Camden High Street, NW1 ☎ 020 7388 3222 🕐 Concerts Sun–Thu. Club nights: Fri–Sat 10pm–4am Ⓜ Mornington Crescent, Camden Town

LONDON COLISEUM

eno.org

London's largest theater (more than 2,300 seats) is home to the English National Opera (ENO). All operas here are sung in English. The English National Ballet and other renowned dance companies perform during breaks in ENO seasons. Guided tours reveal the detail of this beautifully restored Edwardian theater.

➕ K5 ✉ St. Martin's Lane, WC2 ☎ 020 7845 9300 Ⓖ Leicester Square, Charing Cross

LORD'S CRICKET GROUND

lords.org

Lord's is the home of Marylebone Cricket Club, and is where Middlesex play home games in the domestic league. The ground hosts international matches, major finals and T20 games. Tours are available, including the museum.

➕ Off map ✉ St. John's Wood Road, NW8 ☎ 020 7616 8500 Ⓖ St. John's Wood

MINISTRY OF SOUND

ministryofsound.com

Famed for its sound and lighting systems and known as the home of dance and house music, this legendary club—with its own record label—features world-class DJs playing their own unique sets.

➕ N8 ✉ 103 Gaunt Street, SE1 ☎ 020 7740 8600 Ⓖ Tue, Thu–Sat; check for times Ⓖ Elephant and Castle

NATIONAL THEATRE

nationaltheatre.org.uk

Three performance spaces within the National Theatre complex—the Olivier Theatre (seating 1,100 people); the Lyttleton (890); and the smaller Dorfman Theatre (400)—between them stage up to 25 productions a year. They range from re-imagined classics to modern masterpieces and new work by contemporary writers.

➕ L6 ✉ South Bank, SE1 ☎ 020 7452 3000 information, tickets and tours Ⓖ Embankment, Waterloo 🚆 Waterloo

O2 ACADEMY BRIXTON

o2academybrixton.co.uk

South London's popular live music venue attracts big-name bands. It has an art deco interior and room for nearly 5,000 on the huge sloping dance floor. All the big rock bands have played and recorded here.

➕ Off map ✉ 211 Stockwell Road, SW9 ☎ 020 7771 3000 Ⓖ Brixton, Stockwell

O2 ARENA

theo2.co.uk

A music and sports venue in the former Millennium Dome, the O2 Arena has a capacity of 20,000 and hosts big-name concerts, national awards ceremonies, tennis, basketball and darts championships.

➕ Off map ✉ Peninsula Square, SE10 ☎ 020 8463 2000 Ⓖ North Greenwich

---

TICKET TIPS

Use the TKTS half-price ticket booth (in Leicester Square), which has preview and matinée tickets at reduced prices. Many theater box offices sell cheaper tickets from 10am on the day of performance. Go with friends and make a party booking at a reduced rate. Ask the National Theatre, Royal Court and other theaters about special discounts on particular performances; and keep student and senior citizen cards ready. Remember, the show is the same wherever you sit!

The Royal Opera House (roh.org.uk) has 90-minute backstage tours and a 45-minute Velvet, Gilt and Glamour tour. Front-of-house tours of the Royal Albert Hall (royalalberthall.com) last an hour and the guides have some great stories. The National Theatre tours are also good (nationaltheatre.org.uk), and actors reveal history at the Theatre Royal, Drury Lane. Shakespeare's Globe, the Palladium and Coliseum also offer tours.

OLD VIC

oldvictheatre.com

With a history dating back to 1818, this innovative old theater has had some famous artistic directors over the years. It's run as a not-for-profit organization yet has staged many critically acclaimed productions.

M7 · The Cut, Waterloo Road, SE1 · Waterloo, Southwark

THE OTHER PALACE

theotherpalace.co.uk

Opened in 2017, this theater specializes in new musical performances. Its diverse program incorporates cabaret, musical theater and comedy.

G8 · 12 Palace Street, SW1 · 020 7087 7900 · Victoria

THE PHEASANTRY

pizzaexpresslive.com

There's live music every night at this engaging cabaret venue in a historic building that's now home to a Pizza Express restaurant. The performers here know how to please their audiences.

Off map · 152 Kings Road, SW3 · 020 7439 4962 · Sloane Square

PURCELL ROOM

southbankcentre.co.uk

Listen to chamber music, singers, contemporary jazz and poets as well as talks and debates in this intimate space, reopened after extensive refurbishment in 2018.

L6 · South Bank, SE1 · 020 3879 9555 · Embankment, Waterloo

QUEEN ELIZABETH HALL

southbankcentre.co.uk

The fully refurbished concert hall reopened in 2018, with world-class facilities for a regular program of music, spoken word and dance performances.

L6 · South Bank, SE1 · 020 3879 9555 · Embankment, Waterloo

THE RITZ

theritzlondon.com

To enter a bygone world, dress up for dinner and a dance on a Friday or Saturday at London's most opulent dining room (advance booking essential).

G6 · 150 Piccadilly, W1 · 020 7493 8181 · Green Park

RONNIE SCOTT'S

ronniescotts.co.uk

This highly respected jazz club has been staging live acts since 1959, with names such as Miles Davis, Ella Fitzgerald and Buddy Rich performing. Book ahead for its nightly acts or Sunday brunch shows.

J4 · 47 Frith Street, W1 · 020 7439 0747 · Shows daily 7pm; Sunday brunch shows 1–3pm · Tottenham Court Road

ROUNDHOUSE

roundhouse.org.uk

This legendary venue has hosted some of the biggest names in rock

ENTERTAINMENT

and pop music, plus music festivals, dance, circus and cabaret acts, and is recognized for launching the careers of emerging artists.
➕ Off map ✉ Chalk Farm Road, NW1 ☎ 0300 678 9222 🚇 Chalk Farm

ROYAL ALBERT HALL

royalalberthall.com
Opened in 1871, this distinctive round building opposite Kensington Gardens is best known for classical music and pop concerts, opera, ballet and the annual Henry Wood Promenade Concerts (Proms) held nightly from mid-July to mid-September.
➕ B7 ✉ Kensington Gore, SW7 ☎ 020 7589 8212 🚇 South Kensington

ROYAL COURT/JERWOOD THEATRE UPSTAIRS

royalcourttheatre.com
The Royal Court has a lofty artistic reputation and presents only new work by leading or emerging playwrights. John Osborne's ground-breaking *Look Back in Anger* premiered here in 1956.
➕ E9 ✉ Sloane Square, SW1 ☎ 020 7565 5000 🚇 Sloane Square

ROYAL FESTIVAL HALL

southbankcentre.co.uk
This impressive 2,500-seat concert hall, at the heart of the Southbank Centre arts complex, stages large-scale orchestral concerts, jazz, ballet, talks and comedy.

➕ L6 ✉ South Bank, SE1 ☎ 020 3879 9555 🚇 Embankment, Waterloo

ROYAL OPERA HOUSE

roh.org.uk
The world's most acclaimed singers and dancers appear at the opulent Royal Opera House, home to the prestigious Royal Opera and Royal Ballet companies.
➕ K5 ✉ Bow Street, Covent Garden, WC2 ☎ 020 7304 4000 🚇 Covent Garden

SADLER'S WELLS THEATRE

sadlerswells.com
Sadler's Wells is one of the most electrifying dance theaters in Europe, presenting exciting, innovative dance of all genres.
➕ M1 ✉ Rosebery Avenue, EC1 ☎ 020 7863 8000 🚇 Angel

ST. JAMES'S, PICCADILLY

sjp.org.uk
This mid-17th-century church (▷ 73) by Sir Christopher Wren makes a sumptuous setting for lunchtime and evening choral and orchestral concerts.
➕ H6 ✉ 197 Piccadilly, W1 ☎ 020 7734 4511 🚇 Piccadilly Circus

ST. MARTIN-IN-THE-FIELDS

stmartin-in-the-fields.org
Baroque music is the focus of the free lunchtime concerts (Monday, Tuesday and Friday) and candlelit evening concerts (Thursday to Saturday) in this

PUB MUSIC

This can be one of the least expensive and most enjoyable evenings out in London, and worth the trip to an offbeat location. For the price of a pint of beer (usually a huge choice) you can settle down to enjoy the ambience and listen to some of the best alternative music available in town—from folk, jazz and blues to rhythm and blues, soul and much more. Audiences tend to be friendly, loyal to their venue and happy to talk music.

neoclassical church. There's a café/
restaurant in the crypt.

🔡 K5 ✉ Trafalgar Square, WC2 ☎ 020
7766 1100 🚇 Charing Cross

SHAKESPEARE'S GLOBE

shakespearesglobe.com
Plays by Shakespeare and his
contemporaries are performed at
this reconstruction of an open-air
Elizabethan playhouse (▷ 46–
47), from late April to late
September. Tours run year-round.

🔡 P6 ✉ 21 New Globe Walk, SE1
☎ 020 7401 9919 🚇 London Bridge,
Mansion House, Blackfriars, Southwark

THEATRE ROYAL, DRURY LANE

lwtheatres.co.uk
The theater, built in 1812, stages
mostly well-established musicals. It
is believed to be haunted.

🔡 K5 ✉ Catherine Street, WC2
🚇 Covent Garden

VICTORIA PALACE THEATRE

victoriapalacetheatre.co.uk
This century-old theater, splendidly
refurbished in 2017, specializes in
long-running musicals, such as the
major hit *Hamilton*.

🔡 G8 ✉ Victoria Street, SW1 🚇 Victoria

WEMBLEY STADIUM

wembleystadium.com
The world-class football stadium,
home to England matches, also
hosts major rock concerts.

🔡 Off map ✉ Stadium Way, Wembley,
Middlesex ☎ 0800 169 2007. Guided tours
0800 169 9933 🚇 Wembley Park
🚇 Wembley Stadium

WIGMORE HALL

wigmore-hall.org.uk
The hall was built in 1901 as a
recital hall for Bechstein Pianos, so

Wembley Stadium

it has perfect acoustics. It is one of
London's most beautiful settings
for recitals and chamber music,
especially for Sunday concerts.

🔡 F4 ✉ 36 Wigmore Street, W1
☎ 020 7935 2141 🚇 Bond Street,
Oxford Circus

WILTON'S MUSIC HALL

wiltons.org.uk
The world's oldest surviving grand
music hall, tucked away down a
pedestrian alley, is an atmospheric
arts and heritage venue. Its diverse
offering includes classical music,
cabaret, opera, dance and magic.

🔡 Off map ✉ 1 Graces Alley (off Ensign
Street), E1 ☎ 020 7702 2789 🚇 Aldgate
East, Tower Hill

YOUNG VIC

youngvic.org
One of London's most influential
theaters, the Young Vic stages
alternative productions of classics,
new writing and experimental
performances, often with famous
actors taking lead roles.

🔡 M7 ✉ 66 The Cut, SE1 ☎ 020 7922
2922 🚇 Waterloo, Southwark

Eat

There are places to eat across the city to suit all tastes and budgets. In this section establishments are listed alphabetically.

EAT

Introduction

With more than 50 restaurants awarded one or more Michelin stars, the capital's reputation for fine dining continues to grow. Chefs have high profiles and London creates its own culinary trends. Using the finest-quality ingredients, modern British cuisine values simplicity and flavor, innovation and elegant presentation.

Cafés, Brasseries and Pubs

Multicultural London offers exciting restaurants serving a wide variety of different cuisines, ranging from European and cutting-edge contemporary to Indian, Asian and Middle Eastern. Tapas and sushi bars are popular and you don't have to look far to find a good spicy curry or fragrant Thai treat. No longer just an excuse to rest your feet, museum and art gallery cafés are as much of a destination as their exhibitions and, with their all-day menus, convivial brasseries have a relaxed Continental air. Gastropubs combine a fine setting with quality drinks and food.

Restaurant Chains

Try Gourmet Burger Kitchen, Yo! Sushi, Wagamama, Masala Zone and Shoryu Ramen. Zizzi and Pizza Express are good Italian chains.

Afternoon Tea

A great British institution, afternoon tea is widely available in hotels and tearooms from 2 or 3pm. It always includes a pot of tea and something to eat, which can vary from dainty sandwiches and cakes to scones with clotted cream and jam, and often a glass of bubbly.

DRESS CODE

In the past the British loved to dress for dinner, but these days only the most formal restaurants demand a jacket and tie. Customers should dress appropriately, however, to eat in upscale restaurants.

Top to bottom: Olivelli; summertime alfresco dining in the capital; the Dog and Duck: bread stall at Borough Market

EAT

Directory

SOUTH BANK
British and Modern
Aqua Shard
Oxo Tower Bar,
  Brasserie and
  Restaurant
Roast
European
Baltic
Gastropubs/Bars
Anchor Bankside
Anchor & Hope
Lighter Bites
Tate Modern Café

FLEET STREET TO THE TOWER
Asian
Banh Mi Bay
British and Modern
St. John
European
Club Gascon
Gastropubs/Bars
The Peasant
Lighter Bites
The Kitchen
Vegetarian
Vanilla Black

COVENT GARDEN TO REGENT'S PARK
Asian
Benares
Chaopraya Eat-Thai
Diwana Bhel Poori
Masala Zone
Momo
Brasseries/Brunch
Christopher's
Joe Allen
British and Modern
Magpie
Rules
Scotts
European
Herman ze German
Icebar London
Olivelli
Wild Honey
Famous Chefs
Bryn Williams
Gastropubs/Bars
The Dog and Duck
Lowlander Grand
  Café
International
Ceviche
Vegetarian
Wild Food Café

WESTMINSTER AND ST. JAMES'S
Asian
Tamarind
British and Modern
Portrait Restaurant
The Wolseley
Lighter Bites
St. James's Café

AROUND HYDE PARK
Asian
Amaya
Royal China

British and Modern
Bibendum
Maggie Jones's
Famous Chefs
Le Gavroche

FARTHER AFIELD
British and Modern
The Glasshouse
Granger & Co.
Medlar
European
Ottolenghi
La Poule au Pot
Providores & Tapa
  Room
Gastropubs/Bars
The Gun

EAT

Eating A–Z

AMAYA £££

amaya.biz

With a string of positive reviews and a Michelin star, Amaya offers sophisticated Indian grills, exquisitely presented, in a vibrant Knightsbridge setting complete with a theatrical show kitchen.

E8 ✉ Halkin Arcade, Motcomb Street, SW1 ☎ 020 7823 1166 🕐 Mon–Sat 12.30–2.45, 6–10.45, Sun 12.45–2.45, 6–10.15 🚇 Knightsbridge

ANCHOR BANKSIDE £

greeneking-pubs.co.uk

This historic pub with its maze of tiny rooms and pleasant garden terrace enjoys excellent river views. Food is traditional British, with fish and chips and Sunday roasts, but

RIVERSIDE EATING

London is exploiting the potential of its riverside views. As well as traditional pubs such as Anchor Bankside (▷ above) many new restaurants are opening along the South Bank. The most spectacular views are from the Oxo Tower Restaurant (▷ 149) and Tate Modern's rooftop restaurant at Bankside (▷ 151). There are lower but still impressive views from the eateries that line the Thames in the Southbank Centre (▷ 83). The Mayflower, London's oldest Thameside pub (✉ 117 Rotherhithe Street, SE16), is on the original mooring point of the Pilgrim Fathers' ship.

there's also a good selection of lighter dishes.

P6 ✉ 34 Park Street, SE1 ☎ 020 7407 1577 🍴 Restaurant: Mon–Sat 12–10, Sun 12–9 🚇 London Bridge

ANCHOR & HOPE ££

anchorandhopepub.co.uk

A quality gastropub serving good British food. There are no reservations (except for Sunday lunch) so arrive early or be prepared to wait.

M7 ✉ 36 The Cut, SE1 ☎ 020 7928 9898 🕐 Tue–Sat 11–11, Mon 5–11, Sun 12.30–3.15. Dining room opens at 12 for lunch and 6 for dinner; register for first sitting from 5.15 🚇 Southwark, Waterloo

AQUA SHARD £££

aquashard.co.uk

This slick restaurant on level 31 of the Shard serves contemporary British cuisine, but it's the views across the river that are the main draw here. Reserve well ahead.

Q6 ✉ The Shard, 32 London Bridge Street, SE1 ☎ 020 3011 1256 🕐 Mon–Fri 7–10.30am, 12–11pm, Sat–Sun 9am–11pm 🚇 London Bridge

BALTIC £–££

balticrestaurant.co.uk

Head to the bar for cocktails, then on to the dramatic contemporary restaurant for modern Polish and Eastern European food and jazz every Sunday from 7pm.

N7 ✉ 74 Blackfriars Road, SE1 ☎ 020 7928 1111 🍴 Restaurant: Mon–Sat 5.30–11.15, Tue–Sat lunch 12–3, Sun 12–4.30, 5.30–10.30. Bar: 12–12 🚇 Southwark

BANH MI BAY £

banhmibay.co.uk

This bright and light Vietnamese diner in a country-kitchen style is popular with local workers.

AMERICAN EXPERIENCE

America's fast food arrived long before its quality cuisine and restaurant style became established. Better burger chains include The Ultimate Burger and Gourmet Burger Kitchen. Upscale independent options are Joe Allen (▷ 147), Christopher's (▷ below) and PJ's (✉ 52 Fulham Road, SW3 ☎ 020 7581 0025). Other good-value places include The Big Easy (✉ 332–4 King's Road, SW3 ☎ 020 7352 4071), Bodeans (✉ 10 Poland Street, W1 ☎ 020 7287 7575), The Hard Rock Café (✉ 150 Old Park Lane, W1 ☎ 020 7514 1700) and Burger & Lobster (✉ 10 Wardour Street, W1 ☎ 020 3205 8963).

➕ L3 ✉ 4–6 Theobalds Road, Holborn, WC1 ☎ 020 7831 4079 ⏰ Mon–Fri 11.30–3, 5.30–9.45, Sat 12–9.45 🚇 Chancery Lane

BENARES £££

benaresrestaurant.com
Atul Kochhar serves subtly spiced and stylish Indian dishes in his Michelin-starred restaurant. There are particularly innovative vegetarian options.
➕ G5 ✉ 12a Berkeley Square House, Berkeley Square, W1 ☎ 020 7629 8886 ⏰ Mon–Fri 12–2.30, 5.30–10.45, Sat 12–3, 5.30–10.45, Sun 6–9.45 🚇 Green Park

BIBENDUM ££–£££

bibendum.co.uk
In a landmark building with art-nouveau elegance, experience renowned French chef Claude Bosi's flair in the restaurant or go for more relaxed luxury in the Oyster Bar.
➕ D9 ✉ 81 Fulham Road, SW3 ☎ 020 7581 5817; Oyster Bar 020 7589 1480 ⏰ Tue–Wed 6.30–9, Thu–Sun 12–2.15, 6.30–9; Oyster Bar Mon–Fri 8–11, 12–4, 5.45–9.45, Sat 9.30–11.30, 12–4.45, 6–9.45, Sun 9–11.30, 12–4.45 🚇 South Kensington

BRYN WILLIAMS £–££

bryn-somersethouse.co.uk
In a glorious, high-ceilinged dining room, Williams champions dishes from his native Wales, built around fresh, locally sourced fruit and vegetables. The ambience is smart casual, and there's excellent draft beer.
➕ L5 ✉ Somerset House, Strand, WC2 ☎ 020 7845 4646 ⏰ Mon–Fri 12–3, 6–10, Sat 10–4, 6–10, Sun 10–4 🚇 Covent Garden, Charing Cross

CEVICHE ££

cevicheuk.com
Peruvian food is currently a big taste sensation and Ceviche is the hot London source of this tasty and healthy cuisine. Sit at the bar and watch the chefs preparing the ceviche (cured raw fish) dishes.
➕ J4 ✉ 17 Frith Street, W1 ☎ 020 7292 2040 ⏰ Mon–Fri 12–11.30, Sat 10am–11.30pm, Sun 10–10 🚇 Tottenham Court Road, Leicester Square, Piccadilly Circus

CHAOPRAYA EAT-THAI ££

eat-thai.net
Enjoy beautifully presented classic Thai dishes at this quiet, stylish restaurant located just behind Oxford Street.
➕ F4 ✉ 22 St. Christopher's Place, W1 ☎ 020 7486 0777 ⏰ Daily 12–3, 6–11 🚇 Bond Street

CHRISTOPHER'S ££

christophersgrill.com
One of the best places in London for a genuine American brunch,

EAT

Christopher's is in a beautiful Victorian town house in the heart of Covent Garden. The Martini Bar on the ground floor offers burgers and snacks as well as cocktails.
🔲 K5 ✉ 18 Wellington Street, WC2
☎ 020 7240 4222 🕐 Mon–Wed 11.30am–midnight, Thu–Sat 11.30am–1.30am, Sun 11.30–10.30 🚇 Covent Garden

CLUB GASCON £££
clubgascon.com
Good for that special dinner, or afternoon tea with a difference, Michelin-starred Club Gascon serves unusual, robust dishes (including a vegetarian tasting menu) from the southwest of France. Reserve well in advance.
🔲 N3 ✉ 57 West Smithfield, EC1 ☎ 020 7600 6144 🕐 Tue–Fri 12–2, 6–10, Sat 6–10 🚇 Barbican, Farringdon

THE DOG AND DUCK £
nicholsonspubs.co.uk/thedogandducksoholondon
Quality beers, cask ales and hearty pub food feature in this historic Soho pub that boasts of having served John Constable, George Orwell and Madonna.
🔲 J4 ✉ 18 Bateman Street, W1 ☎ 020 7494 0697 🕐 Mon–Thu 11–11, Fri–Sat 11am–11.30pm, Sun 12–10.30
🚇 Tottenham Court Road

DIWANA BHEL POORI £
diwanabph.com
Specializing in authentic Mumbai street food, South Indian *dosas* (crispy filled pancakes) and thalis, this unpretentious, informal Indian restaurant packs in the diners. It's hardly changed for decades.
🔲 H2 ✉ 121–3 Drummond Street, NW1 ☎ 020 7387 5556 🕐 Daily 12–11.30
🚇 Euston, Euston Square

LE GAVROCHE £££
le-gavroche.co.uk
Michel Roux's two Michelin-starred restaurant fuses amazing food, wine and service into an

Fine dining at Le Gavroche

A classic club sandwich

EAT

unforgettable experience.
Reservations are taken three
months in advance.

➕ E5 ✉ 43 Upper Brook Street, W1
☎ 020 7408 0881 🕐 Tue–Fri 12–2, 6–10,
Sat 6–10 🚇 Marble Arch

THE GLASSHOUSE £££

glasshouserestaurant.co.uk
The Glasshouse serves notable
modern dishes, beautifully presented. The wine list is impressive.

➕ Off map ✉ 14 Station Parade, Kew,
TW9 ☎ 020 8940 6777 🕐 Mon–Sat
12–2.30, 6.30–10.30, Sun 7–9
🚇 Kew Gardens

GRANGER & CO. ££

grangerandco.com
Australian chef Bill Granger brings
global tastes and relaxed style to
this all-day eatery in the revitalized
King's Cross Quarter. Eat outdoors
on the piazza in summer.

➕ Off map ✉ Stanley Building, 7 St.
Pancras Square, N1 ☎ 020 3058 2567
🕐 Mon–Sat 7am–11pm, Sun 8am–
10.30pm 🚇 King's Cross, St. Pancras

THE GUN £–££

thegundocklands.com
A popular gastropub on Canary
Wharf, with a long history and
stunning views, the Gun serves
seasonal British food. Seafood and
grills feature on the restaurant
menu, while the pub menu
focuses on British classics.

➕ Off map ✉ 27 Coldharbour, Isle of
Dogs, E14 ☎ 020 7519 0075 🕐 Daily
11.30–11 🚇 Canary Wharf

HERMAN ZE GERMAN £

hermanzegerman.com
Proper German hotdogs made
with homemade sausages from
the Black Forest tempt diners here.

Top your *wurst* with currysauce like
the Germans do and add some
fries on the side.

➕ J5 ✉ 33 Old Compton Street, W1
☎ 020 7734 0431 🕐 Mon–Wed 11–11,
Fri–Sat 11am–midnight, Sun 11–10.30
🚇 Piccadilly Circus, Leicester Square

ICEBAR LONDON ££

icebarlondon.com
Sip a cocktail in London's "coolest"
bar, literally created from ice. Entry
to the bar is by timed ticket for
40-minute sessions. Capes and
gloves are provided. There's a
warm bar, too, and a restaurant
serving modern European food,
including meat and fish dishes
from the coal oven.

➕ H5 ✉ 31–33 Heddon Street, W1
☎ 020 7478 8910 🕐 Opening times vary
🚇 Oxford Circus, Piccadilly Circus

JOE ALLEN ££

joeallen.co.uk
This smart New York-style brasserie
in the heart of Theatreland has
long been popular with actors after
their show. Try the steaks, ribs or
Joe's fishcakes.

➕ K5 ✉ 2 Burleigh Street, WC2
☎ 020 7836 0651 🕐 Mon–Fri 8am–
11.45pm, Sat 9am–11.45pm, Sun
9am–10.30pm 🚇 Covent Garden

THE BILL

When the bill arrives, read it carefully.
A 12.5 percent service charge, or more,
may have been added; if so, there is no
requirement to leave an extra tip. If the
service you received has not been satisfac-
tory, or if you prefer to tip your waiter in
cash, ask them to remove it (tips on your
card may not reach staff directly). Order
tap water if you don't want to feel obliged
to pay for bottled water.

The unmistakable OXO Tower

THE KITCHEN £–££

searcys.co.uk

In the crypt beneath Wren's great St. Paul's Cathedral (▷ 42–43), the coffeehouse offers good-value soup, sandwiches, homemade cakes and hot meals, plus a quiet retreat from the crowds.

🔶 N4 ✉ St. Paul's Churchyard, off Paternoster Row, EC4 ☎ 020 7246 8358 🕐 Mon–Sat 9–4.45, Sun 10–4.30 🚇 St. Paul's

LOWLANDER GRAND CAFÉ £

lowlander.com

This Belgian bar and brasserie is in a great spot for a pre-theater meal on the edge of Covent Garden. Try the Flemish beef stew or rib-eye *steak frites,* followed by decadent thick Belgian waffles.

🔶 K4 ✉ 36 Drury Lane, WC2 ☎ 020 7379 7446 🕐 Mon–Thu 10am–11pm (Wed till 10), Fri–Sat 9am–midnight, Sun 9am–10.30pm 🚇 Covent Garden

MAGGIE JONES'S ££

maggie-jones.co.uk

This cozy Kensington institution is much loved for its informality, excellent wine list and traditional, classic British food.

🔶 Off map ✉ 6 Old Court Place, Kensington Church Street, W8 ☎ 020 7937 6462 🕐 Daily 12–2.30, 6–11 (Sun till 10) 🚇 High Street Kensington

MAGPIE ££

magpie-london.com

This casual, tucked-away eatery in Mayfair, immersed in industrial chic, serves modern British cuisine with creative dishes (from a regularly changing menu) such as squid with grilled turnip and mussel sauce.

🔶 H5 ✉ 10 Heddon Street, W1 ☎ 020 3903 9096 🕐 Mon 5.30–10.30, Tue–Fri 12–2.30, 5.30–10.30, Sat 12–late, Sun 12–4 🚇 Piccadilly Circus

MASALA ZONE ££

masalazone.com

From the creators of Chutney Mary and Veeraswamy, both known for their authentic dishes, comes an informal setting for *thalis* and Indian street food. There are other branches in the capital.

🔶 H5 ✉ 9 Marshall Street, W1 ☎ 020 7287 9966 🕐 Mon–Fri 12–11, Sat 12.30–11, Sun 12.30–10.30 🚇 Oxford Circus

MEDLAR ££

medlarrestaurant.co.uk

Offering imaginative British and European dishes using fresh

SET-PRICE MENUS

Many of London's pricier restaurants offer less expensive set-price menus at lunchtime. Try the three-course Michelin-starred lunch of Hélène Darroze at the Connaught Hotel (🔶 E5 ✉ 16 Carlos Place, W1 ☎ 020 3147 7200) or the lunch menu at Medlar (▷ above).

EAT

seasonal ingredients, this elegant Chelsea restaurant is consistently praised by the critics.

➕ Off map ✉ 438 King's Road, SW10 ☎ 020 7349 1900 🕐 Tue–Sun 12–3, 6–9.30 🚇 Sloane Square, Fulham Broadway

MOMO ££

momoresto.com

In a setting like a Moroccan souk, complete with ornate lamps and low round tables, this is the place for traditional tagines, couscous and slow-cooked lamb dishes, plus excellent meze starters to share. This is a good choice for a romantic dinner, though there's also a basement bar and an informal café next door.

➕ H5 ✉ 25 Heddon Street, W1 ☎ 020 7434 4040 🕐 Daily 12–12 🚇 Piccadilly Circus

OLIVELLI £–££

ristoranteolivelli.co.uk

The flagship venue of London's family-owned Sicilian restaurants, in Bloomsbury, has a regional menu laden with homemade pizza, pasta, meat and fish dishes and delicious desserts.

➕ J3 ✉ 35 Store Street, WC1 ☎ 020 7255 2554 🕐 Mon–Sat 11.30–11, Sun 12–10 🚇 Goodge Street

OTTOLENGHI £

ottolenghi.co.uk

Eating at the famous Israeli chef's Islington outlet is around long communal tables. His Mediterranean-influenced dishes are colorful and full of flavor, with favorites including roast chicken with chilli and basil and roasted sweet potato with pecan and maple syrup.

INDIAN FOOD

London's 2,000 or so Indian restaurants cater to a well-informed local clientele. An Indian meal should have many dishes so, if you are a group, consider making a collective order and sharing. Tandoori dishes (cooked in a clay oven) make good starters. A North Indian meal's main course might include one or two meat offerings, two or three vegetable dishes, rice, a lentil or other pulse, and a variety of breads such as chapati or naan—which are eaten hot, so order more as you go along. Remember the yogurt and pickles, and drink *lassi* (sweet or salty variations on buttermilk/yogurt) or Indian beer.

➕ Off map ✉ 287 Upper Street, N1 ☎ 020 7288 1454 🕐 Mon–Sat 8am–10.30pm, Sun 9am–7pm 🚇 Angel, Highbury & Islington

OXO TOWER BAR, BRASSERIE AND RESTAURANT ££–£££

harveynichols.com

Look out over London while feasting (indoors or out on the balcony) on vibrantly modern British food. Reservations are essential.

➕ M6 ✉ 8th Floor, Oxo Tower Wharf, Barge House Street, SE1 ☎ 020 7803 3888 🕐 Brasserie Mon–Sat 12–11, Sun 12–10; restaurant daily for lunch, tea and dinner 🚇 Blackfriars

THE PEASANT £–££

thepeasant.co.uk

At this friendly gastropub, classic and modern British food, including Sunday roast, is served in the bar, with more sophisticated flavors from the à la carte menu on offer in the upstairs restaurant.

➕ N2 ✉ 240 St. John Street, EC1 ☎ 020 7336 7726 🕐 Mon–Sat 12–11, Sun 12–10.30 🚇 Farringdon

EAT

PORTRAIT RESTAURANT ££–£££

npg.org.uk

Up on level three of the National Portrait Gallery, every table here has a fine London view. Try the chargrilled onglet with Bearnaise sauce for a summer lunch, or come for afternoon tea. Reservations are essential.

➕ J5 ✉ National Portrait Gallery, St. Martin's Place, WC2 ☎ 020 7312 2490 🕓 Times vary 🚇 Leicester Square, Charing Cross

LA POULE AU POT ££

pouleaupot.co.uk

This Belgravia institution is loved as much for its romantic, retro country atmosphere as its classic French cooking. Think bouillabaisse, boeuf bourguignon, cassoulet and tarte tatin. In summer, the outdoor terrace is popular for alfresco trysts. This is the sister restaurant of Maggie Jones's (▷ 148).

➕ Off map ✉ 231 Ebury Street, SW1 ☎ 020 7730 7763 🕓 Daily 12–11 🚇 Sloane Square

PROVIDORES & TAPA ROOM ££

theprovidores.co.uk

Enjoy inventive fusion cooking and New Zealand wines at this friendly Marylebone café, wine bar and fine-dining restaurant. The weekend brunches are highly recommended.

➕ F3 ✉ 109 Marylebone High Street, W1 ☎ 020 7935 6175 🕓 Mon–Fri 8am–10.30pm, Sat 9am–10.30pm, Sun 9am–10pm 🚇 Baker Street

ROAST ££–£££

roast-restaurant.com

Modern British food is served at this restaurant in Borough Market, with many of the seasonal ingredients coming from the market stalls. While you eat, enjoy the views over the market or out toward the Shard and St. Paul's. There's a meaty Sunday lunch, plus a dedicated vegetarian and vegan menu.

➕ Q6 ✉ The Floral Hall, Stoney Street, SE1 ☎ 020 3006 6111 🕓 Mon–Fri 7–10.45, 12–3.45, 5.30–10.45, Sat 8.30–11.30, 12–3.45, 6–10.45, Sun 11.30–6.30 🚇 London Bridge

ROYAL CHINA £–££

theroyalchina.co.uk

Reserve a table or join the long lines for the best dim sum in town, served between 12 and 4.45, at Royal China's flagship branch.

➕ A5 ✉ 13 Queensway, W2 ☎ 020 7221 2535 🕓 Mon–Sat 12–11, Sun 11–10 🚇 Queensway

RULES ££

rules.co.uk

Rules, founded in 1798 and claiming to be London's oldest restaurant, serves traditional English dishes such as oysters, game and pies in plush Edwardian rooms.

➕ K5 ✉ 35 Maiden Lane, WC2 ☎ 020 7836 5314 🕓 Mon–Sat 12–12, Sun 12–11 🚇 Covent Garden

ST. JAMES'S CAFÉ £

royalparks.org.uk

At the heart of St. James's Park, with lovely views to the lake and fountain, this is a great place to unwind at any time of day.

✚ J7 ✉ St. James's Park, SW1 ☎ 020 7839 1149 🕐 Mon–Sat 8–8, Sun 9–8 🚇 St. James's Park

ST. JOHN ££
stjohngroup.uk.com

The robust dishes on offer range from rabbit to oxtail to serious puddings, such as lemon posset.

✚ N3 ✉ 26 St. John Street, EC1 ☎ 020 7521 0848 🕐 Mon–Fri 12–3, 6–11, Sat 6pm–11pm, Sun 12.30–4 🚇 Farringdon

SCOTTS £££
scotts-restaurant.com

Famed for fish and shellfish, with an oyster and champagne bar at its center, this stylish Mayfair favorite entertains meat-lovers too.

✚ F5 ✉ 20 Mount Street, W1 ☎ 020 7495 7309 🕐 Mon–Sat 12–11, Sun 12–10.30 🚇 Bond Street

TAMARIND ££
tamarindrestaurant.com

Contemporary Indian cuisine is impeccably presented in a stylish Mayfair restaurant with a long-held Michelin star. It reopened in 2018 following a major refurbishment.

✚ G6 ✉ 20 Queen Street, W1 ☎ 020 7629 3561 🕐 Daily 12–2.30, 7.30–10.30 🚇 Green Park

TATE MODERN CAFÉ £
tate.org.uk

Take a break from the gallery's art to enjoy upscale café food and Thames views on Level 1 of Tate Modern. For a grander meal, book at the Level 9 Restaurant.

✚ N6 ✉ Tate Modern, Bankside, SE1 ☎ 020 7401 5104 🕐 Daily 10–6 🚇 Blackfriars, Southwark

VANILLA BLACK ££
vanillablack.co.uk

Vanilla Black has a reputation as one of the finest vegetarian restaurants in London, using original flavor combinations created with modern culinary techniques.

✚ M4 ✉ 17–18 Took's Court, EC4 ☎ 020 7242 2622 🕐 Mon–Sat 12–2.30, 6–10 🚇 Chancery Lane

WILD FOOD CAFÉ £
wildfoodcafe.com

This café in Covent Garden calls itself a wellbeing oasis, with a host of innovative raw and plant-based dishes (wholefood, vegan and vegetarian).

✚ K4 ✉ 1st floor, 14 Neal's Yard, WC2 ☎ 020 7419 2014 🕐 Mon 11.30–4, Tue–Sat 11.30–9, Sun 11.30–6 🚇 Covent Garden

WILD HONEY ££–£££
wildhoneyrestaurant.co.uk

Enjoy quality modern European cooking in a stylishly simple Mayfair setting. The set lunch and pretheater menus are especially good value.

✚ G5 ✉ 12 St. George Street, W1 ☎ 020 7758 9160 🕐 Mon–Sat 12–2.30, 6–10.30 🚇 Oxford Circus, Bond Street

THE WOLSELEY ££
thewolseley.com

The Grand Café tradition continues at the Wolseley in Piccadilly, which has an all-day menu with a huge variety. Start the day in art deco grandeur, or relax over afternoon tea after visiting the Royal Academy. Booking is advised.

✚ H6 ✉ 160 Piccadilly, W1 ☎ 020 7499 6996 🕐 Mon–Fri 7am–midnight, Sat 8am–midnight, Sun 8am–11pm 🚇 Green Park, Piccadilly Circus

Sleep

With options ranging from the luxurious to simple budget hotels, London has accommodations to suit everyone. In this section establishments are listed alphabetically.

Introduction

London has many excellent hotels but room rates are very high, and it is certainly worth searching third-party booking websites. You will find weekend and winter rates are often less expensive.

Reservations

Many hotels will ask you to prepay your reservation, or confirm with a credit card, and will charge a fee if you cancel at short notice or fail to turn up. Most hotels have rooms of different sizes, so always ask if there is a choice. Small hotels and guesthouses in historic buildings may not have an elevator.

Outside Central London

If you are prepared to take a slightly longer bus or Tube ride to reach the sights, staying in a residential suburb provides a less expensive alternative to a pricey city-center hotel.

Budget Accommodations

Consider alternatives to hotels, such as renting an apartment, staying in a bed-and-breakfast (B&B) or staying with a family (for online information visit bedandbreakfast.com, athomeinlondon.co.uk or the tourist board's visitlondon.com). During student vacations, inexpensive accommodations are offered by London university halls of residence (see universityrooms.co.uk and ish.org.uk). Youth hostels are another inexpensive option (yha.org.uk).

NOISE LEVELS

As most of London's accommodation options are situated on busy streets, noise can be a problem. Some hotels have double glazing, but that can make rooms unbearably stuffy, especially since air-conditioning is not standard. If you value peace and quiet, look for hotels on side streets in residential areas or request a room at the rear or higher up in the building.

Top to bottom: Charlotte Street Hotel; the grand entrance to The Dorchester; London's top hotels offer superb service; a room at the Charlotte Street Hotel

Directory

SOUTH BANK
Budget
Point A Westminster

FLEET STREET TO THE TOWER
Mid-Range
Chamberlain
Zetter Rooms
Luxury
Andaz
Malmaison
The Rookery

COVENT GARDEN TO REGENT'S PARK
Budget
Morgan Hotel
Mid-Range
Academy
Luxury
Charlotte Street Hotel
Covent Garden Hotel
Hazlitt's
The Principal London
Savoy

WESTMINSTER AND ST. JAMES'S
Luxury
The Goring
The Ritz

AROUND HYDE PARK
Budget
EasyHotel
Kensington House
Pavilion Hotel
Mid-Range
22 York Street
Aster House
The Leonard
My Chelsea
Luxury
The Berkeley
Blakes
The Dorchester
The Halkin

FARTHER AFIELD
Budget
The Beaver
Mid-Range
Henley House
Portobello

Sleeping A–Z

PRICES
Prices are approximate and based on a double room for one night.
£££   over £250
££   £150–£250
£   under £150

22 YORK STREET ££
22yorkstreet.co.uk
This elegant five-story Georgian town house close to Regent's Park has been transformed into a quality bed-and-breakfast.
➕ E3 ✉ 22 York Street, W1 ☎ 020 7224 2990 🚇 Baker Street

ACADEMY ££
theacademyhotel.co.uk
Close to the British Museum, this elegant boutique hotel is set in five restored Georgian town houses.
➕ J3 ✉ 21 Gower Street, WC1 ☎ 020 7631 4115 🚇 Goodge Street

ANDAZ £££
londonliverpoolstreet.andaz.hyatt.com
Casual 21st-century luxury is the theme of this stylishly converted

Victorian railway hotel with a Japanese restaurant, brasserie, English pub and wine lounge.
🚇 R3 ✉ 40 Liverpool Street, EC2 ☎ 020 7961 1234 🚇 Liverpool Street

ASTER HOUSE ££
asterhouse.com
Aster House stands with other chic B&Bs in a smart South Kensington terrace near the museums. You can enjoy the garden and palm-filled conservatory.
🚇 C9 ✉ 3 Sumner Place, SW7 ☎ 020 7581 5888 🚇 South Kensington

THE BEAVER £
beaverhotel.co.uk
The Beaver offers B&B accommodation on a tree-lined Victorian crescent in Earl's Court, near South Kensington's museums.
🚇 Off map ✉ 57–59 Philbeach Gardens, SW5 ☎ 020 7373 4553 🚇 Earl's Court

THE BERKELEY £££
the-berkeley.co.uk
Guests at this luxury Knightsbridge hotel enjoy traditional elegance, plus famed service and food. Facilities include a spa, rooftop pool and two great restaurants.
🚇 E7 ✉ Wilton Place, SW1 ☎ 020 7235 6000 🚇 Hyde Park Corner, Knightsbridge

LOCATION
It is well worth perusing the London map to decide where you are likely to spend most of your time. Then select a hotel in that area or accessible to it by Underground on a direct line, so you avoid having to change trains. London is vast and it takes time to cross, particularly by bus and costly taxis. By paying a little more to be in the heart of the city, you will save on travel time and costs.

BLAKES £££
blakeshotels.com
Designer Anoushka Hempel has achieved sumptuous decadence in this South Kensington boutique hotel, attracting a celebrity guest list. There's a stunning restaurant, a stylish bar and a tranquil courtyard.
🚇 Off map ✉ 33 Roland Gardens, SW7 ☎ 020 7370 6701 🚇 South Kensington, Gloucester Road

CHAMBERLAIN £–££
thechamberlainhotel.co.uk
In lavishly converted 20th-century offices in the City of London, this hotel has comfortable bedrooms, some with a roof terrace. Its popular pub serves craft beer on tap.
🚇 S5 ✉ 130–135 Minories, EC3 ☎ 020 7680 1500 🚇 Aldgate, Tower Hill

CHARLOTTE STREET HOTEL £££
firmdalehotels.com
Close to London's theater district, Kit and Tim Kemp's boutique cocktail of comfort and fairy-tale Englishness offers individually designed rooms and a restaurant with a Bloomsbury Group theme.
🚇 H3 ✉ 15 Charlotte Street, W1 ☎ 020 7806 2000 🚇 Goodge Street

COVENT GARDEN HOTEL £££
firmdalehotels.com
Another stylish Kemp boutique hotel, complete with wood-paneled drawing room and library, the Covent Garden's location and deluxe rooms attract celebrities.
🚇 J4 ✉ 10 Monmouth Street, WC2 ☎ 020 7806 1000 🚇 Leicester Square

THE DORCHESTER £££
dorchestercollection.com
The Dorchester is one of London's finest hotels. Deliciously art deco,

it is a London landmark from its grand entrance and piano bar to the Oliver Messel suite, from the luxurious spa to the famous Grill. It boasts the only UK hotel restaurant with three Michelin stars.

➕ F6 ✉ Park Lane, W1 ☎ 020 7629 8888 🚇 Green Park, Hyde Park Corner

EASYHOTEL £

easyhotel.com

EasyHotel is inexpensive and very basic. The rooms are tiny, many without a window, but all come with a shower room. There is no provision for meals on site, and TV and internet access are extra.

➕ A8 ✉ 14 Lexham Gardens, W8 ☎ Reserve by website only 🚇 Earl's Court, Gloucester Road; other locations available

THE GORING £££

thegoring.com

High standards of old-fashioned hospitality and service make this splendid hotel memorable. Its gorgeous private gardens are a great setting for afternoon tea.

➕ G8 ✉ 15 Beeston Place, SW1 ☎ 020 7396 9000 🚇 Victoria

THE HALKIN £££

comohotels.com/thehalkin

With a stylish blend of Western and Asian aesthetics, the contemporary design of this luxury boutique hotel extends to its spa and Michelin-starred Spanish restaurant.

➕ F7 ✉ 4 Halkin Street, SW1 ☎ 020 7333 1000 🚇 Hyde Park Corner

HAZLITT'S £££

hazlittshotel.com

The 23-room Hazlitt's has near-perfect period decoration in three 18th-century houses, and is superbly located for Theatreland.

SLEEP

The Covent Garden Hotel dining room

157

➕ J4 ✉ 6 Frith Street, W1 ☎ 020 7434 1771 🚇 Tottenham Court Road

HENLEY HOUSE £–££

henleyhousehotel.com
In this boutique hotel the decor is light and modern, the facilities are good and breakfast is served in the garden conservatory.
➕ Off map ✉ 30 Barkston Gardens, SW5 ☎ 020 7370 4111 🚇 Earl's Court

KENSINGTON HOUSE £–££

kenhouse.com
This beautifully restored 19th-century property provides contemporary accommodations in the heart of Kensington. Its 41 bedrooms are light and stylish.
➕ A7 ✉ 15–16 Prince of Wales Terrace, W8 ☎ 020 7937 2345 🚇 High Street Kensington

THE LEONARD ££–£££

theleonard.com
A discreet, small hotel, the Leonard personifies traditional classic elegance. The spacious rooms, suites

The Savoy, a byword for luxury

and family rooms are comfortable and there's a good restaurant.
➕ E4 ✉ 15 Seymour Street, W1 ☎ 020 7935 2010 🚇 Marble Arch

MALMAISON ££–£££

malmaison.com
In Malmaison's signature edgy decor, the rooms in this converted former nurses' home are stylishly contemporary—all stripped wood floors, exposed brick walls and moody lighting—as is the Chez Mal brasserie.
➕ N3 ✉ 18–21 Charterhouse Square, EC1 ☎ 020 3750 9402 🚇 Farringdon

MORGAN HOTEL £

morganhotel.co.uk
Reserve ahead for this small, friendly family-run hotel set over two Georgian buildings near the British Museum.
➕ J3 ✉ 24 Bloomsbury Street, WC1 ☎ 020 7636 3735 🚇 Tottenham Court Road, Russell Square

MY CHELSEA ££

myhotels.com/chelsea
The cool, clean lines of urban chic and a relaxed color scheme distinguish this small neighborhood hotel. Tanya's restaurant on the ground floor offers wholesome, artisanal meals.
➕ D9 ✉ 35 Ixworth Place, SW3 ☎ 020 7225 7500 🚇 South Kensington, Sloane Square

PAVILION HOTEL £

pavilionhoteluk.com

Behind a plain facade lie 30 eccentric, brightly colored themed rooms in a hotel that describes itself as "fashion rock 'n' roll."

➕ C4 ✉ 34–36 Sussex Gardens, W2 ☎ 020 7262 0905 Ⓜ Paddington

POINT A WESTMINSTER £

pointahotels.com

The rooms may be compact in this new hotel chain, but they are bright and modern, the beds are comfortable, the bathrooms have power showers and WiFi is free.

➕ M8 ✉ 118 Westminster Bridge Road, SE1 ☎ 020 7633 9317 Ⓜ Lambeth North

PORTOBELLO ££–£££

portobellohotel.com

In this romantic Notting Hill retreat, each charming room has a distinct personality and the elegant Sitting Room enjoys views over the private gardens.

➕ Off map ✉ 22 Stanley Gardens, W11 ☎ 020 7727 2777 Ⓜ Notting Hill Gate

THE PRINCIPAL LONDON £££

phcompany.com

This new hotel in a century-old building in Bloomsbury is all about grace and glamor, blending Victorian touches with a contemporary feel. There are excellent dining venues on site.

➕ K2 ✉ 1–8 Russell Square, WC1 ☎ 020 7123 5000 Ⓜ Russell Square

THE RITZ £££

theritzlondon.com

Guests enjoy sumptuous luxury, with traditional style, gilt decor and the great first-floor promenade to London's most beautiful dining room, overlooking Green Park.

➕ G6 ✉ 150 Piccadilly, W1 ☎ 020 7493 8181 Ⓜ Green Park

THE ROOKERY £££

rookeryhotel.com

Full of period charm with wood paneling, open fires and antique furniture, there's a club-like atmosphere in this boutique hotel.

➕ N3 ✉ 12 Peter's Lane, Cowcross Street, EC1 ☎ 020 7336 0931 Ⓜ Farringdon

SAVOY £££

fairmont.com/savoy-london

A top-to-toe refurbishment has brought this grand London hotel, right on the Thames, firmly into the 21st century while preserving the grand Edwardian decor. Its wining and dining options include the American Bar.

➕ L5 ✉ Strand, WC2 ☎ 020 7836 4343 Ⓜ Covent Garden

ZETTER ROOMS ££–£££

thezetter.com

In a clever repurposing of a Victorian warehouse, the rooms have mood lighting and workstations, raindance showers and duck-down pillows.

➕ N2 ✉ St. John's Square, 86–88 Clerkenwell Road, EC1 ☎ 020 7324 4444 Ⓜ Farringdon

BARGAIN LUXURY

To be pampered amid sumptuous surroundings may be an essential part of your trip. London's most luxurious hotels have been built with no expense spared. Hotel prices are generally very high, but it's always worth asking when you make your reservation whether any special deals are available. Most deluxe and mid-range hotels offer weekend deals throughout the year.

Need to Know

This section takes you through all the practical aspects of your trip to make it run more smoothly and to give you confidence before you go and while you are there.

NEED TO KNOW

Planning Ahead

WHEN TO GO

London is busy year-round, and most attractions remain open all year. Peak season is from April to September, when you should arrive with a hotel reservation and theater tickets. The quietest months are January to March and November, when hotels may give a discount.

TEMPERATURE

JAN	FEB	MAR	APR	MAY	JUN	JUL	AUG	SEP	OCT	NOV	DEC
42°F	45°F	50°F	55°F	63°F	68°F	72°F	72°F	66°F	57°F	50°F	45°F
6°C	7°C	10°C	13°C	17°C	20°C	22°C	22°C	19°C	14°C	10°C	7°C

Spring (March to May) has a mixture of sunshine and showers, although winter often encroaches on it.

Summer (June to August) can be unpredictable, with clear skies and hot days interspersed with rain, sultry grayness or thunderstorms.

Autumn (September to November) often has clear skies that can feel almost summery. Real autumn starts in October, and colder weather sets in during November.

Winter (December to February) is generally fairly cold, and snow can sometimes disrupt public transportation.

WHAT'S ON

January *Sales:* Shopping bargains at stores all over the city.

January/February *Chinese New Year:* Dragon dances and fireworks in Chinatown.

March *London Beer Week:* Hop-tastic events in pubs and pop-ups.

April *Oxford and Cambridge Boat Race* (1st Sat): This famous race takes place on the Thames from Putney to Mortlake. *London Marathon:* 40,000 runners zigzag through the capital.

May *Chelsea Flower Show:* One of the world's best shows takes place at the Royal Hospital, Chelsea.

June *Trooping the Colour* (2nd Sat): The "Colours" (flags) are trooped before the Queen on Horse Guards Parade, Whitehall. *Wimbledon* (Jun/Jul): The world's leading grass-court tennis tournament.

July *BBC Proms* (Jul–Sep): Nightly classical concerts in the Royal Albert Hall and other venues.

August *Notting Hill Carnival* (last weekend): Europe's biggest carnival, with floats, music and costumes.

September *Totally Thames Festival* (all month): Arts, culture and river events along London's 67km (42-mile) stretch of the Thames.

October *Museums at Night* (last weekend): Out of hours celebration. *BFI London Film Festival:* Films, documentaries and shorts from around the world.

November *Bonfire Night* (5 Nov): Bonfires and fireworks marking the failed Gunpowder Plot of 1605. *Lord Mayor's Show:* The City's favorite ritual, with parades and pageantry in a long procession.

December *Christmas music* (all month): Festive music in churches and many concert halls.

LONDON ONLINE

visitlondon.com
London's official site is up-to-date and comprehensive with ideas for museums, theater and restaurants, and sections for children and visitors with disabilities. It also offers discounts.

royalparks.org.uk
From Greenwich Park to Green Park, all eight of London's Royal Parks are detailed here, with information on special events, facilities and activities for children.

tfl.gov.uk
Transport for London's official site gives ideas for what to see and do, ticket information for the Underground, buses, DLR and river services. It also has a WAP-enabled journey planner.

royal.gov.uk
The official site of the British royal family, with history, royal residences, who's doing what today and a monthly online magazine.

weknowlondon.com
You can book hotels, tickets to attractions and theaters, tours and day trips, and order sim cards for collection at Heathrow airport.

londontown.com
This comprehensive site covers what's on, what's new, attractions, events, theaters, sightseeing ideas, traditions, nightlife, shopping, markets and general advice.

hrp.org.uk
This site is dedicated to London's five great historic palaces, from the Tower of London to Hampton Court Palace.

officiallondontheatre.co.uk
The Society of London Theatre's official site, with all the latest theater news, together with interviews with stars, performance details, information about discounted tickets and theater access for visitors with disabilities.

TRAVEL SITES

nationaltrust.org.uk
This independent organization owns and maintains many buildings and extensive lands, some of them in and around London.

english-heritage.org.uk
English Heritage is responsible for many historic sites and buildings—with ideas for days out in London.

fodors.com
A complete travel-planning site. You can research prices and weather, book air tickets, cars and rooms, pose questions (and get answers) from fellow travelers, and find links to other sites.

visitbritain.com
Great places to visit around the UK, with accommodations, transport, special offers and travel tips.

INTERNET ACCESS

All of the capital's public libraries have internet facilities. WiFi is available at airports, train stations and in the majority of cafés. Most hotels have WiFi or modem plug-in points (data ports) in rooms and public areas.

Getting There

TRAINS

● For all information, visit National Rail at nationalrail.co.uk.

● Purchase tickets at the station or online at nationalrail.co.uk or thetrainline.com.

● All major London train stations are on Tube lines.

● There are eight major London train stations and sometimes a town is served by more than one.

● Fares are high but deals are available if you book in advance and can be flexible. If you are traveling extensively with other family members, look into special railcards.

NIGHT BUS

The N9 night bus connects Heathrow with central London (Trafalgar Square) and leaves from the Central Bus Station (for Terminals 2 and 3) and Terminal 5 about every 20 minutes. The journey time is around 1 hour 15 minutes.

BY COACH

If you travel to London by long-distance coach you will probably arrive at Victoria Coach Station (VCS) on Buckingham Palace Road, which is very near Victoria train and Tube station. Alternatively, there is a taxi rank immediately outside.

AIRPORTS

Heathrow and Gatwick are the principal airports serving the city. However, Stansted, Luton and London City are increasingly busy with traffic from Continental Europe. There are train links to the Continent via Lille and Paris and road links to Channel ports.

60km (40 miles)

Luton Airport
Bus 1hr 30 min
Train 25 min

Stansted Airport
Bus 1hr 40 min
Train 40 min

London City Airport
Bus 25–40 min
DLR/Underground 25 min

Heathrow Airport
Bus approx 1hr
Train approx 15 min
Underground 1hr

Gatwick Airport
Bus 1hr 30 min–2hr 45 min
Train 30 min

FROM HEATHROW

Heathrow (heathrow.com) has four terminals (Terminals 2, 3, 4 and 5), 24km (15 miles) west of central London; all are well served by public transport. The Tube's Piccadilly line runs from 5am to 11.40pm (Terminal 4 station closes Mon–Sat 11.35pm, Sun 11.15pm) and takes about an hour. On Fridays and Saturdays there's a 24-hour service from Terminals 2 and 3 and Terminal 5. The Heathrow Express (heathrowexpress.com), a high-speed rail link to Paddington station, runs from 5.10am to around 11.40pm every 15 minutes. Prices are high for the 15-minute journey. A cheaper alternative is the TfL Rail local stopping service (tfl.gov.uk) to Paddington station; journey time 30–50 minutes.

National Express (nationalexpress.com) coaches run from around 4.30am to 10pm to Victoria Coach Station; the average journey time is around 75 minutes. Taxis wait outside the terminals; the trip takes under an hour, depending on traffic, and costs £50–£70.

FROM GATWICK

Gatwick airport (gatwickairport.com) is 48km (30 miles) south of central London and the best way to reach the city is by train. The Gatwick Express (gatwickexpress.com) train leaves for Victoria Station every 15 minutes, (5.51am–11.20pm) and takes 30 minutes. Southern (southernrailway.com) runs slightly slower but cheaper services to Victoria, and Thameslink (thameslinkrailway.com) goes to London Bridge and King's Cross/St. Pancras International. Taxis cost more than £100.

FROM STANSTED

Stansted airport (stanstedairport.com) is 56km (35 miles) northeast of central London. The Stansted Express (stanstedexpress.com) to Liverpool Street Station takes around 50 minutes. Several bus/coach operators run services to Liverpool Street and Victoria stations. Journey time is up to 1 hour 40 minutes. A taxi costs from £100.

FROM LUTON AIRPORT

Luton airport (london-luton.co.uk) is 53km (33 miles) north of London. There are bus links to Victoria Coach Station, taking around 1 hour 30 minutes, and East Midlands and Thameslink trains to St. Pancras International, taking from 40 minutes. Taxis cost about £80.

FROM LONDON CITY AIRPORT

City Airport (londoncityairport.com) is at Royal Albert Docks, 14km (9 miles) east of central London. Trains from London City Airport Docklands Light Railway (DLR) station feed into the Underground system. Taxis from the terminal cost around £35.

THE CHANNEL TUNNEL

Eurostar train services (eurostar.com) connect Britain to Continental Europe, and are a great way of arriving in London, or for taking trips out to Paris, Brussels and elsewhere in Europe. The journey to Brussels takes about 2 hours, Paris about 2 hours 15 minutes.

Trains depart from St. Pancras International terminal, close to King's Cross station. Eurotunnel (eurotunnel.com) is for vehicles only. Fares are lower if you reserve ahead.

CROSSRAIL

Crossrail (crossrail.co.uk) is a huge civil engineering and transport infrastructure project that's scheduled to begin operating (as the Elizabeth line) in 2020. The high-speed service will link 40 stations (including Heathrow Airport) across the capital. In the meantime, you will see signs of the massive construction in various parts of the city, some of which may lead to public transport route changes and road closures.

LOST/STOLEN PROPERTY

Even the most seasoned traveler occasionally leaves something behind—airlines find forgotten computers almost daily.
● Contact the place where you think you left it or saw it last.
● Report the loss to a police station and get a copy of the report form for your insurance claim.
● If you lose your passport, report it to the police and your embassy immediately. Provided you have photocopies of the key pages, it should not be difficult to replace but there's usually a charge.
● Contact for London Transport and taxi lost property (☎ 0343 222 1234, tfl.gov.uk).

Getting Around

DRIVING TIP

Driving in London is slow, parking is expensive and fines are high. Congestion charges operate from Monday to Friday, 7am–6pm, costing £11.50 a day. Do not drive in London unless you have to; use the Tube or bus instead.

VISITORS WITH DISABILITIES

London is steadily improving its facilities for visitors with disabilities, from shops and theaters to hotels and museums. Newer attractions such as Tate Modern and the London Eye are better equipped than ancient buildings such as Westminster Abbey. Check out the London Tourist Board's comprehensive website (visitlondon.com) and guide books, such as *Access in London* (published by Access Project PHSP; accessinlondon.org). Also consult Can Be Done (canbedone.co.uk) and Dial (scope.org.uk/dial). DisabledGo (disabledgo.com) has information on accessible places to visit in the UK with a good section on London. William Forrester, a lecturer and wheelchair user, leads tailor-made tours in the city (☎ 01483 575401).

Underground trains (known as the Tube) and buses run from around 5am to just after midnight, when service is via night buses. The Tube runs a 24-hour service on Fridays and Saturdays. The transport system is divided into zones (clearly marked on transport maps) and you must have a ticket valid for the zone you are in.

THE UNDERGROUND (TUBE)

Eleven color-coded lines link almost 300 stations. The network also includes the Docklands Light Railway (DLR) and London Overground rail, which covers large parts of the city as well as many suburban areas.

BUSES

Plan your journey using the latest copy of the Central London bus guide, available at London Transport information centers or at tfl.gov.uk. Bus stops are indicated by a white sign with the red Underground logo; many now have display panels with real-time arrivals information. Note that you can no longer pay cash on London buses, so you will need to buy a Travelcard or Oyster card, or use a contactless UK-registered bank card (some international cards, including Amex and Mastercard, also work).

TAXIS

Taxis that are available for rental illuminate a yellow "For Hire" sign on the roof. Hold out your hand to hail them beside the road. Drivers of official cabs will know the city well. They are obliged to follow the shortest route unless an alternative is agreed beforehand. A "black cab" (now often not black) is licensed for up to five passengers. Meter charges increase in the evenings and at weekends. Take care using minicabs, as they may have no meter and inadequate insurance. Call a black cab via Computer Cab (tel 020 7908 0271, comcablondon.com).

TRAVEL INFORMATION CENTERS

These sell travel passes, provide Tube, train and bus route maps and information on cheap tickets, and open daily at the following stations:

Heathrow terminals 2 and 3, Gatwick Airport, Liverpool Street, Victoria, Euston, King's Cross, Paddington and Piccadilly Circus. For Transport for London services, call 0343 222 1234.

PAYING FOR TRAVEL

Travelcards, valid after 9.30am (you must pay a surcharge to use them earlier) for unlimited travel by Tube, railway, Docklands Light Railway and buses, are sold at travel information centers, railway and Tube stations, and some shops. They cover travel for one day or seven days.

Oyster prepay smartcards are valid for use on the Underground, DLR, bus, Thameslink and some national rail networks. Single fares are much cheaper with Oyster than cash, and the cards can be topped up with more credit. You can buy a visitor Oyster card before arriving in the UK by visiting the Transport for London website (tfl.gov.uk).

You can also pay for journeys with a contactless debit or credit card, or a mobile payment app on your smartphone. This works exactly like an Oyster card—simply touch the card or your phone to the card reader on the ticket barrier on entry and exit and the correct fare will automatically be deducted. If you make multiple journeys, the total cost will be capped at the cost of a Travelcard, so there is no risk of overpaying.

LONDON PASS

This pass (londonpass.com) offers free entry to more than 80 top attractions and fast-track entry to save you time. It's valid for 1, 2, 3, 6 or 10 consecutive days and prices start at £62 for a one-day adult pass.

BOATING AND BIKING

Thames Clippers (thamesclippers.com) runs a commuter, leisure and sightseeing service aboard high-speed catamarans.

London Cycling Campaign (lcc.org.uk) can advise on biking in the capital. You can rent a bicycle from, and return it to, one of the many Santander Cycles project docking stations scattered across London (tfl.gov.uk).

TIPS

● London is huge. It may take more than an hour to reach your destination, so allow plenty of time—and plan your day to avoid crisscrossing the city.
● When buying a Travelcard, select the appropriate pass for the areas you will visit. A card covering Zones 1 and 2 is usually adequate; pay a supplement if you go outside this area.
● Use common sense when traveling alone at night, but there is no need to be unduly concerned.
● Smoking and vaping are banned on all public transportation.

FUN TOURS

Below are some ideas for quirkier ways to explore.
● London Walks (☎ 020 7624 3978, walks.com).
● Open House Architecture (☎ 020 3006 7008, open-city.org.uk).
● By water (▷ 54–55).
● Cable car (☎ 0343 222 1234, emiratesairline.co.uk). The Emirates Air Line is a cable car across the Thames between North Greenwich and the Royal Docks. It offers easy access to the O2 Arena with great views. The rides are approximately 10 minutes each way, shorter during rush hour.

NEED TO KNOW

Essential Facts

VISAS AND TRAVEL INSURANCE

Check visa and passport requirements before traveling; see fco.gov.uk or ukinusa.fco.gov.uk. EU citizens are likely to be covered for medical expenses with an EHIC card until 2020, but adequate travel insurance is still strongly advised and is essential for visitors from outside the EU.

MONEY

The pound sterling (£) is the official currency in the UK. There are bank notes in denominations of £5, £10, £20 and £50, and coins in £1 and £2 and 1, 2, 5, 10, 20 and 50 pence.

CREDIT CARDS

● Credit cards are widely accepted. Visa and MasterCard are the most popular, followed by American Express, Diners Club and JCB. Credit cards can also be used for withdrawing cash from ATMs (though this is pricey).
● If your credit cards are lost, report each one immediately to the credit card company and, if stolen, the police as well. For your credit card company's local 24-hour emergency number, go to ukphonebook.com. It's free but you have to register.

ELECTRICITY

● Standard supply is 240V. Motor-driven equipment needs a specific frequency; in the UK it is 50 cycles per second (kHz).

EMERGENCY TELEPHONE NUMBERS

● For police, fire or ambulance, call 999 from any telephone, free of charge. The call goes directly to the emergency services. Tell the operator which street you are on and the nearest landmark, intersection or house number. Stay by the telephone until help arrives.

MEDICAL TREATMENT

● EU nationals and citizens of some other countries with special arrangements (Australia and New Zealand) may be eligible to receive free National Health Service (NHS) medical treatment provided that they are in possession of the correct documentation (EHIC for EU visitors); this may change after the UK leaves the EU in 2019.
● All other visitors have to pay.
● If you need an ambulance call 999 on any telephone. For advice in less urgent cases, call 112.
● NHS hospitals with 24-hour emergency departments include: University College Hospital, 235 Euston Road, NW1, tel 020 3456 7890; St Mary's Hospital, Praed Street, W2, tel 020 3312 6666; St Thomas' Hospital, Westminster Bridge Road, SE1, tel 020 7188 7188.
● Private hospitals, with no emergency unit, include the Cromwell Hospital, 164–178 Cromwell Road, SW5, tel 020 7460 2000.
● Dental problems: Call the NHS free helpline (tel 111) to find a walk-in center. You don't need an appointment for these but the wait can be long. King's College Hospital, Denmark Hill, SE5, has an Acute Dental Care clinic for treating serious dental problems (helpdesk tel 020 3299 1919, Mon–Fri 8.30–12.30).
● Eye specialist: Moorfields Eye Hospital, City Road, EC1, tel 020 7566 2345 is for sight-threatening emergencies only. Some opticians offer same-day repairs for glasses.

MEDICINES

● Many drugs cannot be bought over the counter. For an NHS prescription, you pay a modest flat rate; if a private doctor prescribes, you pay the full cost. To claim charges back on insurance, keep receipts.

● Chemists that keep longer hours include: Boots, 44–46 Regent Street, Piccadilly Circus, W1, is open until 11pm (midnight Fri–Sat, 7pm Sun), tel 020 7734 6126; Boots, 114 Queensway, W2, tel 020 7229 1183, is open until midnight (6pm Sun); Zafash, 233–235 Old Brompton Road, SW5, tel 020 7373 2798, is open daily 24 hours.

OPENING HOURS

● Major attractions: Seven days a week; some open late certain days of each week.

● Shops: Generally Mon–Sat 9.30/10am–6pm; department stores until 8 or even 10pm (Selfridges, Oxford Street). Many shops open Sun 12–5/6pm; department stores have browsing time before the tills open from 11.30am. Late-night shopping (until 8pm) is on Thu in the West End and Wed in Knightsbridge.

● Banks: Mon–Fri 9.30–5; a few remain open later or open on Sat mornings. *Bureaux de change* generally have longer opening hours. ATMs are abundant.

● Post offices: Usually Mon–Fri 9–5.30, Sat 9–12.30.

NEWSPAPERS AND MAGAZINES

Newspapers include *The Financial Times*, *The Daily Telegraph*, *The Guardian*, *The Daily Mail* and *The Times*; Sunday papers include *The Sunday Times*, *Sunday Telegraph* and *The Observer*. Free papers (Mon–Fri) are *Metro* and the *Evening Standard*, which is strong on entertainment and nightlife (standard.co.uk). The free magazine *Time Out* (timeout.com), published weekly on Tue), lists almost everything going.

TIPPING

Many restaurants add a 12.5 percent service charge. For taxis, hairdressers and other services, 10 percent is acceptable. Tips are not usual in theaters or concert halls, or in pubs (unless there is table service).

EMBASSIES

Australian High Commission	✉ Australia House, Strand, WC2 ☎ 020 7379 4334, uk.embassy.gov.au
Canadian High Commission	✉ Canada House, Trafalgar Square, SW1 ☎ 020 7004 6000, canadainternational.gc.ca
New Zealand High Commission	✉ New Zealand House, 80 Haymarket, SW1 ☎ 020 7930 8422, mfat.govt.nz
Embassy of Portugal	✉ 11 Belgrave Square, SW1 ☎ 020 7235 5331, londres.embaixadaportugal.mne.pt
Embassy of Spain	✉ 39 Chesham Place, SW1 ☎ 020 7235 5555, exteriores.gob.es
Embassy of the US	✉ 33 Nine Elms Lane, SW11 ☎ 020 7499 9000, uk.usembassy.gov

MAILING A LETTER

Stamps are sold at post offices, supermarkets and some newsagents and shops. Trafalgar Square Post Office stays open late:
✉ William IV Street, WC2
🕐 Mon–Fri 8.30–6.30 (Tue from 9.15), Sat 9–5.30.
Mailboxes are red.

TELEVISION

● The five most-watched channels in Britain are BBC1, BBC2, ITV1, Channel 4 and Channel 5. The BBC is funded by a licence fee and there is no advertising on any BBC channels.
● Television channels available in hotel rooms will be at least the above and most likely digital terrestrial and satellite services, with a large number of channels and a wide variety of content. Programs can also be viewed on the internet and 4G cellphones.

STUDENTS

Holders of an International Student Identity Card (ISIC) will be able to obtain some good concessions on travel and entrance fees.

PHONES

● London numbers (eight digits) are prefixed with the code 020 when dialing from outside the city. To call London from abroad, dial the country code 44, then just 20, then the eight-digit number.
● Public phones accept coins, phonecards and credit cards.
● For the operator tel 100. For the international operator or to reverse charges tel 155.
● Directory enquiries: There are many options; tel 0800 953 0720 for details and prices.
● To make international calls from the UK, dial 00, then the country code (1 for the US and Canada).
● Beware of high charges on numbers that start with 084, 087 or 09.
● Numbers starting 0800 are free.
● Before departure, consult with your cell/mobile phone provider on coverage and rates.

PUBLIC HOLIDAYS

● 1 Jan; Good Fri; Easter Mon; May Day (first Mon in May); last Mon in May; last Mon in Aug; 25 Dec; 26 Dec.
● Almost all attractions and shops close Christmas Day; many close 24 Dec, 1 Jan, Good Fri and Easter Sun as well. Some shops, restaurants and attractions remain open throughout, but check.

SENSIBLE PRECAUTIONS

● Keep valuables in a hotel or bank safe box.
● Note all passport, ticket and credit card numbers, and keep separately. Carry photocopies of the key pages of your passport.
● Make sure that bags are fully closed and keep them in sight at all times—do not put them on the floor or over the back of a chair.
● Exercise caution when traveling, particularly after dark, and keep to streets that are well lit. If using a taxi, use a black cab, or ask your hotel or restaurant to book one for you.

TOURIST INFORMATION

● There are tourist information centers all over London. Check visitlondon.com for locations.

Books and Films

London's vitality, variety, glamor and squalor have always provided rich pickings for writers and filmmakers.

London is steeped in history, and acclaimed historian Peter Ackroyd's books are an involving way to get beneath the city's skin. Try *London, The Concise Biography* (2012). The updated *London: A Life in Maps* by Peter Whitfield (2017) is full of intriguing facts and insights; Lucy Inglis has entertaining revelations in *Georgian London: Into the Streets* (2014) while *Literary London* by Eloise Millar and Sam Jordison (2016) reveals the stories behind the writers, from Chaucer to the modern day.

For a quirky angle on the capital, look for *Walk the Lines* (2013), in which trivia-fan Mark Mason tells how he walked the entire length of the London Underground, overground. In *Spitalfields Life* (2013), lively pen portraits chronicle daily happenings around this revitalized area of east London. *The Zoo: The Wild and Wonderful Tale of the Founding of London Zoo* by Isobel Charman (2016) is an amazing story, full of incredible Victorian characters, human and animal.

FILMS

A Street Cat Named Bob (2016) is a feel-good tale of an ex-heroin addict who finds fame busking around Covent Garden with a stray cat. *The Lady in the Van* (2015), with its wonderfully eccentric main character, is also a quintessentially London film. James Bond's adventures in *Sceptre* (2015) were set partly in the British Intelligence building on the Thames and climaxed on Westminster Bridge. *London Town* (2016) harks back to the punk era of the 70s, while *Kids in Love* (2016) reveals the city's bohemian side. Action thriller *London Has Fallen* (2016) has scenes shot at Somerset House, as does *Darkest Hour* (2017), the story of Churchill's early days in power at the start of World War II, where it stands in for Buckingham Palace. *Prince of Thieves* (2018), about a daring 2015 heist in the Hatton Garden jewelry district, has aerial shots of the city.

LONDON CLASSICS

Perhaps the most famous book about London is *The Diary of Samuel Pepys*, in which the observer, Pepys, recorded events from 1600 to 1669. Many of Charles Dickens' novels have London settings, including *Oliver Twist* (1837), *The Old Curiosity Shop* (1840), *Bleak House* (1853) and *Little Dorrit* (1857). In 1887, Sir Arthur Conan Doyle introduced his character Sherlock Holmes in the novel *A Study in Scarlet*. The legendary fictional detective lived at 221b Baker Street, W1. In William Thackeray's *Vanity Fair* (1847), Becky Sharp begins her adventures in Russell Square. Humorist P.G. Wodehouse, creator of the eccentric Jeeves and Wooster, based his Drones Club on several London gentlemen's clubs of the time (1920s). *84 Charing Cross Road* (1982), a memoir of warm, funny and sad letters between New Yorker Helene Hanff and London antiquarian bookseller Frank Doel during the 1940s, is a modern classic that made a memorable movie.

Index

We would like to thank the following photographers, companies and picture libraries for their assistance in the preparation of this book.

All images are copyright AA/James Tims and Sarah Montgomery except:

3iii AA/R. Mort; 6c Benjamin John/Alamy Stock Photo; 6/7t GeoPic/Alamy Stock Photo; 6/7tc Kathy deWitt/; Alamy Stock Photo; 6/7b Stuart Forster/Alamy Stock Photo; 7c Bombaert Patrick/Alamy Stock Photo; 8/9i Liberty London; 8/9iv © Science Museum Group; 8/9vi AA/N. Setchfield; 10br The Art Archive/Alamy Stock Photo; 11bl Mary Evans Picture Library/ Alamy Stock Photo; 12 AA/N. Setchfield; 15tl AA/N Setchfield; 17tr courtesy Royal Collection 2011, Her Majesty Queen Elizabeth II/Derry Moore; 17c Monica Wells/TTL; 18l Lea Hughes/ Alamy Stock Photo; 18c Nick Malsen/Alamy Stock Photo; 18/9t © England's Historic Cities/© Michael Heffern/London and Partners; 18/9c © England's Historic Cities/© Stephen McLaren/ London and Partners; 19r © England's Historic Cities/© Michael Heffern/London and Partners; 20 National Maritime Museum; 21tr National Maritime Museum; 21cl AA/S and O Mathews; 21c National Maritime Museum; 26 © Historic Royal Palaces; 26/7 © Historic Royal Palaces; 27tr © Historic Royal Palaces; 28 courtesy Harvey Nichols; 29tl courtesy Swarovski/Yellow Door; 29tr Travelshots.com/Alamy Stock Photo; 29cl courtesy Harvey Nichols; 30 courtesy EDF Energy London Eye/British Tourist Authority/James McCormick; 31tl courtesy EDF Energy London Eye; 31tr courtesy EDF Energy London Eye; 31c courtesy EDF Energy London Eye; 32/33tl courtesy Museum of London; 34 Ronald Weir/TTL; 35tr courtesy The National Gallery; 36 courtesy The National Portrait Gallery; 37tl courtesy The National Portrait Gallery/Andrew Putler; 38tr/39tl AA/M. Jourdan; 38l courtesy Natural History Museum; 38cr/39cl courtesy Natural History Museum; 39tr courtesy Natural History Museum/D. Adams; 40 David Noton/ TTL; 41tr SJ Images/Alamy Stock Photo; 42l © England's Historic Cities/© Cultura Creative 2012/London and Partners; 42tr/43tl Courtesy St Paul's Cathedral/Graham Lacdao; 44l Courtesy Science Museum © Plastiques Photography; 44br/45bl © Plastiques Photography, courtesy Science Museum Group; 45r courtesy Science Museum/© Jody Kingzett; 46l AA/R. Turpin; 46/47 James Barrett/Alamy Stock Photo; 48l Skate at Somerset House with Fortnum & Mason © James Bryant and Somerset House; 48/9c The Edmond J. Safra Fountain Court at Somerset House © Jeff Knowles and Somerset House; 49tl Artist Charles Jeffrey at Somerset House Studios © Dan Wilton and Somerset House; 52tl AA/N. Setchfield; 53tr Switch House, Tate Modern © Iwan Baan; 54t/55tl AA/C. Sawyer; 54cl AA/T. Woodcock; 55 Thames River Services; 56 © Tower Bridge; 57t © Tower Bridge; 57c © Tower Bridge; 59tr © Historic Royal Palaces/Richard Lea-Hair; 60t/61tl Maurice Crooks/Alamy Stock Photo; 61tr courtesy; V & A Museum/Alan Williams; 61cr courtesy V & A Museum/Hufton Crow; 62tl Tom Mackie/TTL; 64t AA/R. Mort; 66br Bank of England; 68b AA/N. Setchfield; 69bl Gareth Gardner; 70b AA/S. McBride; 71b AA/N. Setchfield; 72bl Postal Museum; 74br Sir John Soane's Museum/Photo Gareth Gardner; 76bl AA/P. Kenward; 76br Courtesy Museum of London; 78bl AA/D. Forss; 78br Warner Bros. Studio Tour London—The Making of Harry Potter; 79bl AA/W. Voysey; 82br AA/M. Jourdan; 83cl AA/R. Turpin; 83br courtesy EDF Energy London Eye; 87 *The Golden Hinde*; 88tr AA/N. Setchfield; 88b courtesy Museum of London; 89b AA/W. Voysey; 92tr courtesy Museum of London; 92ct Courtesy St Paul's Cathedral/Peter Smith; 92cb © Tower Bridge; 94l N. Setchfield/Alamy Stock Photo; 94b The Edmond J. Safra Fountain Court at Somerset House © Jeff Knowles and Somerset House; 98tr AA/N. Setchfield; 98br © England's Historic Cities/© Stephen McLaren/London and Partners; 100t courtesy The National Portrait Gallery/Andrew Putler; 101t London Stills; 101bl City Cruises; 104ii © England's Historic Cities/© Julian Love/London and Partners 104iii; London Stills; 104vii AA/N. Setchfield; 104viii AA/B. Smith; 106l courtesy V & A Museum; 110i AA/P. Kenward; 110ii AA/P. Kenward; 110iii; AA/T. Woodcock; 10v courtesy Victoria and Albert Museum/Morley von; Sternberg; 112t AA/S and O Mathews; 112br David Noton/TTL; 113t AA/S and O Mathews; 113cl AA/W. Voysey; 116tr Rik Hamilton/Alamy Stock Photo; 120/121ii AA/P. Kenward; 120/121iii AA/R. Turpin; 120/121iv AA/R. Strange; 120/121v AA/M. Trelawny; 125br Fortnum & Mason; 127br Liberty London; 130/131iii AA/M. Jourdan; 139 Brian Anthony/Alamy Stock Photo; 140 Charlotte Street Hotel; 142i © Olivelli; 142ii AA/M. Jourdan; 142iii Dog and Duck Pub; 146bl Le Gavroche, Issy Croker; 146br AA/N. Setchfield; 148 AA/N. Setchfield; 152 AA/R. Mort; 154i AA/W. Voysey; 154iii OneOff Travel/Alamy Stock Photo; 154iv VIEW Pictures Ltd/Alamy Stock Photo; 157 Covent Garden Hotel

Every effort has been made to trace the copyright holders, and we apologize in advance for any unintentional omissions or errors. We would be pleased to apply any corrections in a following edition of this publication.

London 25 Best

WRITTEN BY Louise Nicholson and Sue Dobson
UPDATED BY Emma Levine
SERIES EDITOR Clare Ashton
COVER DESIGN Jessica Gonzalez
DESIGN WORK Liz Baldin
COLOR REPROGRAPHICS Ian Little

Published in the United Kingdom by AA Publishing.

ISBN 978-1-6409-7208-7

FIFTEENTH EDITION

Printed and bound in China by 1010 Printing Group Limited

10 9 8 7 6 5 4 3 2 1

A05671
Mapping © Crown copyright and database rights 2019 Ordnance Survey. 100021153.

Titles in the Series